The Economics of Bureaucracy:

An Academic View On Why Government Sucks

Daniel Rothschild

The Economics of Bureaucracy

Daniel Rothschild

Table of Contents

The Economics of Bureaucracy

Foreword

This book is a tour de force of libertarianism. But not just of any old version of the freedom philosophy, of which there are many. This perspective, predicated upon the non-aggression principle and private property rights based on homesteading, ranges widely. It stretches all of the way from the classical liberalism of Milton Friedman and Friedrich Hayek, which allows all sorts of government interventionism in the economy up to the minarchist very limited government views of scholars such as Robert Nozick, Ayn Rand, Ron Paul and Ludwig von Mises, and finally reaches the apex in the anarcho-capitalist views of Murray Rothbard. For Rothschild, there is only one pure version of this perspective; that of the latter.

Our author is equally radical when it comes to economics. Not for him any "market failures" of the sort claimed by most mainstream economists. If you want to read an utter and total evisceration of monopoly, externalities, public goods as requiring statist amelioration, you will find that all here.

Think that patents and copyrights are required if we are to have significant innovation and invention? Thanks to this book, you can think again. Our author offers solid evidence to the contrary: scientific, musical and other advances in the absence of propertizing the unpropertarianable. But his case against intellectual property is by no means limited to the pragmatic or utilitarian. He also drives home the deontological point that if someone steals your shoes, salad or shirt, you no longer have them. But if another person makes use of your idea, you still have it available to you. Hence, stealing is not an appropriate description of what is going on when patents are violated.

In the view of most people, seemingly sophisticated political analysts unfortunately included, law and government are invariably linked, sort of like love and marriage, or horse and carriage. In a particularly brilliant chapter on this subject, Rothschild puts paid to all of that.

He demonstrates, superlatively, that not only is this not the case, but that all too often the state is the main enemy of just law. Indeed, governments, even apart from the wars they continually engage in, have murdered far more of their citizens than any other institution known to man.

An oft heard objection to all programs of privatization is "how will the poor pay for these goods and services, without the all-loving state to pay for them?" One answer is that under laissez faire capitalism, while relative poverty cannot of course be ended (as long as there is any inequality whatsoever), the absolute variety thereof most certainly can. Wealthier is healthier, and if there is one thing that free enterprise does is promote economic development. Then, too, protection would be given to all and sundry by wealthy people who own streets, highways, parks, museums, shopping centers, and in whose interest it is to ensure that all customers are safeguarded. Rothschild insightfully harkens back to yet another refutation of this objection: "A possible objection to private law enforcement is that it would favor the wealthy, and poor people who could not afford protection would be left defenseless. The Icelandic system of law enforcement had a way to solve this problem with transferable tort claims. If one did not want to seek damages himself he could sell his tort claim to someone else and that person would be able to seek damages on his behalf. Such a system allows those who are too weak or too poor to sell their torts to those who are more willing and able to seek justice on their behalf."

Let me save the best for the last. In two excellent chapters, the author of this book utterly destroys Ronald Coase and his world-famous (well, within economic circles) theory of social costs. He does so on several grounds, one of which is that justice consists not of looking back in time and seeing who did what to whom, but, rather, looking toward the future and awarding property or rights under dispute to whichever party can best enhance overall wealth with it. This is obnoxious, evil, a moral abomination. A rapist can be set free, even awarded damages and court costs, if he can prove that he enjoyed this despicable act more than the harm perpetrated upon, felt by, his victim. Why is it so important that this theory be taken down a peg or two or three? Surely, there are more contemptible theories than this one (Naziism, Communism). This is due to the fact that everyone full well knows, or at least really should know, that these other theories are indeed disgraceful. Coase is different, far different. Rather than seen as wicked, he is viewed as a heroic economist by his professional peers. He even won a Nobel Prize (1991) in this discipline. Readers of this book should be grateful to its author for exposing the fallacies of this highly regarded economist.

Unlike some authors, Rothschild gives credit where credit is due. Original thoughts of his abound but he quotes widely from the libertarian and Austrian economics literature, and cites many other writers. That, too, is to his credit.

If you are interested in coverage of the entire waterfront of radical libertarianism, or anarcho-capitalism, along with a good dose of Austrian economics, this is the book for you.

- Walter E. Block

The Economics of Bureaucracy

Introduction

Hello and welcome to the wonderful and sexy world of economics, politics, and comparative institutional analysis. In the following book, there are nine essays on political theory using economics to explain human behavior and one chapter on what an anarchist constitution might look like. As you will learn, economics is all about people responding to incentives. Good incentives produce good results, and bad incentives produce bad results. In order to have a good outcome, one doesn't need good people, but good incentives. People are only as good or bad as the incentives they face. Understanding this important lesson makes all talk of voting for the good guy (or the lesser of two evils) meaningless. If the incentives don't change, neither will the results and waiting in vain for moral leaders is simply a waste of time. If you want better political outcomes, there must be better political incentives. We cannot simply hope for good people to begin working for the government or running for political office.

Most of the following essays deal with economics applied to politics and the government and use the lessons of economics to see why government bureaucrats act the way they do. The government, much like soylent green, is made of people. And people's behavior is easy to predict once one understands the incentives they face because people generally act the same when the incentives are the same.

Using a few rules of economics, we can apply them to different areas to predict how people behave and then use empiricism to illustrate such truths. For example, one such economic rule is what is known as price theory, which states that there is an equal relationship between price and supply and an inverse relationship between price and demand, with all else remaining equal. In other words, when the price increases, supply increases along with it while demand decreases. Conversely, when the price decreases, supply decreases along with it, and demand increases.

One illustration of this theory happens when a minimum wage law is implemented. When the price of labor increases as a result of minimum wage legislation, the supply of labor increases because higher wages incentivize more people to enter the workforce, and demand for labor services decreases since the price of labor is now more expensive. The result of this is a surplus of labor, or in other words, unemployment. Another illustration of price theory involves laws prohibiting the sale of organs. When the price of organs decreases all the way down to zero, the number of people willing to supply organs decreases, and the demand for organs increases. The result is a shortage of organs (like kidneys) for people who need them, or in other words, death, since people who need the organs to live do not get them. One last illustration of price theory is seat belt laws. When the cost (or price) of dying from a seat belt decreases as a result of seat belt laws, the demand of people wanting to drive faster increases. The result: More car accidents and pedestrian deaths. Once one understands price theory, one can apply it to all sorts of interesting topics and the results will always be the same: cost and price move in the same direction as supply, and cost and price move in the opposite direction as demand.

Another important lesson of economics is the importance of competition and dispersed knowledge. All businesses want to act as exploitative monopolists, but competition and the freedom to compete prevents them from being too greedy. A free market is not a naïve belief that businessmen are noble people, (most are probably not) but an understanding that competition is the solution to achieve noble outcomes. Take dispute resolution as an example. The government (which is a monopolist in the area of dispute resolution) doesn't want there to be a decrease in crime because a decrease in crime means less demand for their services, which means more people resisting tax hikes. As you will see in my essays on police and civil asset forfeiture, police unions lobby to increase the number of actions that are considered crimes in order to artificially drum up more demand for their services. They don't actually have to decrease crime and be effective since there are no competitors doing a better job, since competition has been restricted by the state. If there were competition in dispute resolution, each individual firm may want there to be more crime to create more demand for their services, but since there is competition, if the firm doesn't actually lower the crime rate for the individuals who hire them, such individuals would find a firm that does. In other words, while each individual firm would like to act like the government and create more crime, competition forces them to behave and not do so. This is not to say that crime is a creation of the state. Even in the state's absence, crime would still exist, it would likely just be lower, but still with us since human beings are not angels, and many humans have a demand to commit crimes.

The following book (excluding the first chapter, which explores what an anarchist constitution might look like) has one essay on anarchism and compares it with the state and shows that people fare better when their society is stateless than when their society has a state (government). This is not to say that all stateless societies are better than societies with a government since many stateless societies have backward and communistic social norms that lead to perverse results. All that I'm saying is that in the same society with the same social norms, people will do better if that society decides to get rid of its government and embrace anarchy. Certain anarchist societies would be more desirable than others, much like some societies with a state are more desirable than others. What matters most are the social norms in that society. A society with social norms of collectivism and distrust of markets will be unlikely to produce good results, no matter what type of social institution they live under. One cannot force freedom on people who do not want it. Whereas a society of individualism and a love of markets is likely to thrive, even with a government violating their rights. They would just thrive even more if the government was not stealing, imprisoning, or murdering them.

For those interested, I don't go into the morality of anarchism. This is not because I oppose morality, but because I'm more interested in a scholarly empirical analysis than I am in a moral one. Also, I don't know if I even subscribe to the morality that many people use to advocate for individualist anarchism known as the non-aggression principle, which states that aggression (which is the initiation of physical force) is never justified, and since the state commits aggression, the state is therefore morally unjustifiable. While I am sympathetic to the non-aggression principle, I view it more as a good rule of thumb than a hard and fast rule. I agree with economist Bryan Caplan that if you can't think of exceptions to the non-aggression principle (or any principle for that matter), then you aren't trying hard enough. I think there are some situations (albeit rare) when aggression is justified. Even so, this does not justify political authority. The state is not morally justified for many reasons, but because it commits aggression is not one of them. Most reasonable people believe that if committing a small number of aggression results in stopping a large amount of aggression then committing that small amount of aggression is justifiable. I think I agree with most people on this issue. My morality is common sense, even if my political conclusions are radical.

My main goal in publishing this book is to make money. My second goal is to get those who read it to think like economists, understand price theory, the importance of competition and dispersed knowledge, and understand that incentives are what matter, not good people. Morality is overrated. Give me good incentives any day. With that said, I hope you enjoy reading this book as much as I enjoyed writing it. Now move your ass and get to reading!

A Somewhat Anarchistic Constitution

We the students of Professor Foldvary's class, in order to get a more perfect grade, establish this Constitution to protect life, liberty, and property.

The following Constitution of Libertopia was formed to separate ourselves from the United States of America. Because the United States government has shown themselves to not represent our needs and to be abusive, we establish the following Constitution to be bound by the citizens of Libertopia. The area of Libertopia includes 13 states that decided to secede from the United States. The states that comprise Libertopia are 1) Texas, 2) Utah, 3) New Hampshire, 4) Tennessee, 5) Oklahoma, 6) North Dakota, 7) South Dakota, 8) Colorado, 9) Idaho, 10) Alaska, 11) Missouri, 12) Virginia, and 13) Georgia.

Section 1: All legislative powers are those that are mentioned in the Constitution. There will be no new laws enacted. The only laws which the people of Libertopia are bound by are those which are in the Constitution. Any rules and laws that are not in the Constitution are delegated to the people themselves, where any new law which is enacted must require the consent of 100% of the population. This is because the Constitution adheres to natural laws. People's rights are not subject to a vote and therefore any new law which is enforced must attain the consent of 100% of the population of Libertopia. The only laws which don't require 100% consent are those which are consistent with natural law (e.g. a rapist, murder or thief doesn't have to consent to the prohibition on rape, murder, or theft).

Section 2: All of the rules prescribed in the Constitution will be enforced by private firms. In order to have a real separation of powers, instead of splitting the government into different branches, those which enforce the law and those which enact the law are totally separate. Since a government which levies taxes is a monopoly, in order to ensure a true separation of powers, no branch of government will enforce the Constitution. The following laws are laws that the people of Libertopia agree to be bound by so they know what the laws are, but who enforces them will be left up to the individuals to decide.

Section 3A: The state does not have the power to levy and collect taxes. Since taxation itself is coercive and the Constitution is meant to be a voluntary contract, there shall be no taxes. Those that wish to have certain services be socialized may fund such programs via lottery or any other non-coercive means. The winner of the lottery will receive 10% of the winnings and the remaining 90% will fund the various government departments.

Section 3B: There shall be two areas which will be socialized and governmental. The funds to pay for these two branches shall be funded by a voluntary lottery, user fees, or other non-coercive means. The two departments which will be governmental are:

1) The department overseeing applications for citizenship of Libertopia. Each of the 13 states will have at least one department to secure citizenship. The fee will be small and affordable (under a $1,000) to obtain citizenship and if one can't afford to pay for the fee, such a fee will be waived if a person agrees to serve on a jury within the next three months or agrees to work in community service (such as working in the department that determines citizenship itself) in order to compensate the government for the fee and

2) A court which shall have only one very specific purpose: to fine other courts for not granting defendants a trial within one week of arrest or indictment. If it is determined that the court is expanding its power, the people of Libertopia have a right to vote the people in the court system out of office at any time, subject to a majority vote. The majority of each state may vote on whether to remove the judges. If it can be proven by a private court that this court is exceeding its power and is legislating from the bench, private courts have a right to take action against the court and fine the government court for acting outside its

own boundaries. A private court, which is fined by the government court for violating the right to a speedy trial, may not take action against the government court due to inherent bias, but other private courts not subject to the suit may bring a suit against the government courts if they have evidence to prove that the government court is exercising powers beyond their one delegated authority.

Section 3C: As discussed in Section 3A, the funds that the states receive will be voluntary and used only to pay for limited services. Individuals shall not be prevented from organizing and raising funds for services as long as coercion is not utilized. Anyone who prefers not to participate in some or all parts of the Libertopia retains the right to withdraw from any part of society and from any government programs. In order to determine which services are socialized, a supermajority of 80% of each state must approve of the decision. The socialized functions can either be provided by the all 13 states, by the individual states, or a few states may want to join in a union and socialize some of these functions together. There will be a meeting once a year on July 4th to vote on whether more services should be voluntarily socialized. It's important to note that these services, while socialized, are not truly governmental in the sense that the government may not prevent competition or interfere with the free market in any way at any time. (For example, if people want transportation to be "publicly" provided, this doesn't mean that private transportation companies are forbidden from competing with them or that the funds will be paid for by taxation. All it means is that if some states decided to socialize the costs—either by having user fees or by having a lottery—they may do so, but they may not prevent competition.) Certain services may not be socialized at any time, even with a supermajority vote.

Section 3D: The following are services which may never be socialized and will remain totally private and open not only to competition, but to the profit and loss system without having to rely on guaranteed funds from the government:

A) Schools shall never be socialized. No governing body of Libertopia shall have any involvement in school standards, licensing, or provide any funding to schools. Education is too important to be politicized and subject to favoritism or rent-seeking. Education thrives when there is competition (just like everything else). While the authors of this Constitution would like there to be competition in all areas and to have no company operate without being totally funded by the consumer, we also understand that there are some people who don't feel the same way. We also understand that no one has a right to make others victims of their own actions and delegate the rights of others to be subject to their wishes. Since school involves teaching children who are unable to consent, to have a vote on how they will be educated when they can't vote is unfair. Likewise, school is too important to have universal standards (whether the standards are universal across states or in a single state).

B) There shall be no central bank. Money is too important to be left into the hands of any central authority and therefore money will be provided by the free market. Let money be open to competition. No majority has a right to vote on how to control the money. Central banking is a crime. Any state which attempts to maintain statist institutional versions of banking will be fined and brought to a private court.

C) Besides having one court collect fines to ensure a speedy trial, the court will be limited to that function. There will be no governmental legislative, judicial, or executive branch and there will be no government courts. As the United States demonstrated, no government could truly have a separation of powers. State departments are willing to allow governmental overreach and allow for presidential executive orders. There can never be a separation of powers if the government itself is able to judge its laws. A kangaroo court is where the judge is both lawmaker and executioner and as such, governmental courts are forbidden. There will be no Supreme Court. The courts will be subject to the market. Judge's rulings may always be challenged and the accused always has a right to go to another court and challenge the court's verdict. Since the judge's salary is dependent on the court remaining in business, and the only way to ensure that the judge isn't protected by legislating from the bench is to allow courts to go out of business and the only way to do that is to have a free market court system, instead of a governmental court system where going out of business is harder (though not impossible if secession is legal and there is no taxation).

Section 4: A person has a right to his property and to his life. There will be no victimless crimes. ALL acts between consenting adults are permissible.

Section 5: If a person violates another person or his property, the victim may take the person who violated his person or property to court. If the victim is unable to bring the aggressor to court, the victim's heirs may bring charges against the aggressor. If the victim has no family and friends and the victim is unable to delegate a proxy in his stead, anyone may bring a suit against the aggressor.

Section 6: There will be criminal trials and civil trials. Both trials will follow the same format in terms of establishing guilt and the jury process. The difference between a civil and criminal penalty is the degree of the crime. For any violations of a person's body, the violator will be charged in a criminal court. For damage to a person's property, the victim is entitled to monetary restitution. Since the victim is the one bringing the complaint, it is up to the victim to decide if he wants to turn a criminal case into a civil case and collect torts instead of seeking a criminal penalty.

Section 7: A jury will be composed of 12 men. The members of the jury will be selected by random lots. There will be no voir dire process, lest the jury's randomness be compromised. The judge, defense, and prosecutors may not question the jury to see if they have any biases. The jury will be selected at random. The reason there will be no voir dire is because this is viewed by Libertopia as jury tampering, done in order to get certain people on the jury and to weed certain people out. Such a process is viewed by the people of Libertopia as having a biased jury. The compensation for jury members will be determined by private courts. A person on a trial which is over swiftly will not be required to be a jury member more than once a year. People who are selected for jury duty on trials that last over 2 months will not be required to attend jury duty for another 5 years.

Section 8: The accused has a right to a speedy trial and will face trial as soon as he is brought to court. In order to ensure that a person isn't waiting indefinitely for a trial, the longest a person can be waiting for a trial is one week. After the accused is charged with a crime and arrested he will be tried ideally right away and maximum no longer than a week. Any court which waits longer than a week to try the accused shall be fined $1,000 per day after the one-week period. The full time from arrest until sentencing shall count as time served towards the sentence if sentenced to incarceration.

Section 9: All people have a right to a trial and to be judged by a jury of their peers. If a person would rather be judged without a jury, he may waive such a right and receive a trial with one or more judges. Defendants in civil and criminal cases shall receive a trial, even in cases involving confessions or plea deals. History has shown that defendants are often coerced to plead guilty or confess to crime in an effort to avoid the harshest penalties. The logic for everyone being tried is to prevent abuse by the authorities trying to bully the accused into admitting guilt. We understand that people often claim to be guilty of a crime they didn't commit in order to avoid a harsher sentence. We are also aware that people can be bullied into saying they are guilty when they are not. In order to prevent such abuse, even if a person says he is guilty he will have a right to a trial in order to ensure he is guilty and not just saying he is to secure a lighter sentence. If one says they are guilty and admits his crime or turns himself in to the authorities such noble actions will be taken into account when passing sentencing.

Section 10: The people of Libertopia admit humility and therefore don't have any rule stipulating how payment of a trial is settled. Does the guilty party pay everything, including the lawyer, judge, jury, and prison fee? Does each party split the costs evenly? We admit to not knowing such answers and leave these decisions to the various courts. Each court may decide for themselves how exactly trials should be funded.

Section 11: Thomas Jefferson once said, "*God forbid we should ever be 20 years without such a rebellion. The people cannot be all, & always, well informed. The part which is wrong will be discontented in proportion to the importance of the facts they misconceive. If they remain quiet under such misconceptions it is a lethargy, the forerunner of death to the public liberty. We have had 13 states, independent 11 years. There has been one rebellion. That comes to one rebellion in a century & a half for each state. What country before ever existed a century & half without a rebellion? & what country can preserve it's liberties if their rulers are not warned from time to time that their people preserve the spirit of resistance? Let them take arms.*" We agree with such a sentiment. Therefore every 20 years, the people of Libertopia will meet to discuss whether the Constitution should be altered or if there should be a new one. All the people of Libertopia, ages 16 and up will meet and convene and there will be a vote where a super-majority of 80% is needed to determine if there should be a new Constitution and new laws. If a person doesn't want to attend the 20 year meeting—which will meet on the first Monday after 20 years have passed— he may delegate a proxy, which has to demonstrate proof of being a proxy by having a signed document, phone number, and address of the person for which he is a proxy.

Section 12: The people of Libertopia are advocates of free banking. Legal tender laws are completely forbidden. No branch of the government is in charge of coining money or having an "independent" central bank control the money on their behalf. Money is too important to be left in political hands. This specific section of the Constitution shall not be amended. No votes can decide to control the flow and supply of money. There will be free banking, where the type of currency used, the amount of reserves being held in banks will be determined by the free market and not by the government.

Section 13: We the people of Libertopia advocate open-border immigration. No passports are required to enter the land. People own their own property and no one may immigrate into a person's home without his consent, but any area of Libertopia which is not privately owned (either through homesteading or inheritance) will be free for immigration and homesteading.

Section 14: If a foreign-born person aged 16 years or older wishes to become a citizen of Libertopia, they may apply for citizenship. There will be a "Department of Naturalization" where a person can apply to be a citizen. Each of the 13 states of Libertopia will have at least one "Department of Naturalization" in their state. The department will have certain standards for determining whether to grant or revoke citizenship. The rules are as follows:

    A) If a person wants to renounce their citizenship at any time, they are free to do so.

    B) In order to obtain citizenship, a criminal background check will be required. If the person obtaining citizenship is a repeat offender of crimes and the crimes he committed involved real human victims (i.e. violated natural law—were acts which are coercive and violate a person or his property) he will be denied citizenship. We understand that people err and if on determining his background check, if he is not a repeat offender for violent crimes, his acceptance for citizenship will be decided based on a majority vote by the citizens of whichever state of Libertopia he decides to emigrate to.

C) There will be a small fee to obtain citizenship of Libertopia.

Section 15: Consistent with the name of our country, we don't advocate slave contracts and believe in secession down to the individual. A person has a right to secede. States have a right to secede from any country or union, counties have a right to secede from the states, and streets have a right to secede from the counties. In order to secede from Libertopia, all a person has to do is announce his secession two weeks in advance to the "Department of Naturalization" located in the state where he resides. If a person secedes from Libertopia, he will not be protected by the country of Libertopia, but he is free to find some other agency to defend him and protect him without having to leave his home. If a person commits physical invasion against another or engages in theft or fraud, he will be subject to punishment and the laws of Libertopia will apply to him, even if he has seceded. Secession means that a person isn't required to serve jury duty or pay any fee that a new Constitution may compel the citizens of Libertopia to pay. Just because a person secedes from a country doesn't mean he can commit acts of violence without repercussions. If a person commits acts of physical aggression, the victim, the victim's heirs, or anyone who bought a transferrable tort claim may seek damages against the aggressor who decided to secede. If the aggressor does not comply with the just ruling against him for a truly criminal act, force may be used against him to attain his compliance. Secession shall not be allowed to grant immunity to persons who commit crimes against people or their property.

Section 16: Pollution may be considered an act of physical invasion and therefore a person has a right to seek compensation and charge any polluter for physically damaging a person or his property with pollutants. Acts of pollution are subject to a liability rule where the polluter pays the victim of his pollution based on the damage he caused. A third party arbitrator will judge what the damage to the pollution will be. The third party arbitrator is one in which both the defendant and the plaintiff agree to. If the defendant (i.e. the polluter) fails to be subject to any of the third party arbitrators that are available—the prosecutor (i.e the victim of pollution) will be able to choose a third party of his choice to assess damages, even against the will of the polluter. Such a ruling will be done in order to ensure compliance and to penalize the accused for not being willing to cooperate and abide by a third party of his choice when given the chance.

Section 17: The Constitution of Libertopia is based upon a respect for individual rights. This is why the only actions which are forbidden are physical invasions. There are no victimless crimes, there are no taxes, immigration isn't restricted, and there are no 'crimes against society'. If a person strikes another in the face, he didn't hurt "society's nose" he hurt the nose of the person he struck in the face. Therefore, there is no prosecuting attorney by the state. The prosecutor is the victim, the victim's heirs or the victim's representative agents. The state may not claim to be the victim's representative agent, the victim himself must select his proxy. If the victim has no family and friends, a person is free to homestead his claim and seek justice on the victim's behalf, but the state may not. However, if the victim forgives the aggressor and doesn't wish to press charges such wishes must be respected and no charges will be levied against the accused, though coercion by the aggressor to attain forgiveness shall be dealt with harshly.

Section 18: Many people claim to want laws limited to preventing violence against another and yet what is considered "violence' and aggression is continually expanded. There are so many laws against preventative crimes that many people are needlessly incarcerated for fear that such a person may one day commit a crime. It is for this reason that the Constitution of Libertopia only advocates "ex post" rules instead of an "ex ante" system.

Instead of having numerous laws to "prevent" harm (like laws which make it a crime to speed because the driver may get into an accident), the only laws that are forbidden are ex post rules. We understand that some of the 13 states want their own Constitution and their own laws instead of having this Constitution bound by the 13 states of Libertopia. We respect the right of states to draft their own Constitution as long as the laws they enact don't violate the rules that are in this Constitution, which means for instance, since the Constitution of Libertopia says a person may not be charged with a victimless crime, no state has a right to enact victimless crime laws. But each of the 13 states do have a right to enact rules that aren't recognized by the Federal Constitution of Libertopia as long as the rules don't go against this Federal Constitution of Libertopia. Since the Federal Constitution doesn't prohibit ex-post laws, if each state wants to draft their own Constitution and have an ex-ante system of law or both an ex-post and ex-ante system of law, the states are free to do so. If a person decides to secede from a state or moves to another state and the state he moves to doesn't recognize the other states ex-ante laws, he is not bound by them. Such a ruling allows different states to experiment, while also providing a loophole for people who consider ex-ante laws a violation of their freedom by being able to move out of the state where they reside. Also, since there are private roads, issues such as drunk driving and speeding will be decided not based on state or the federal government but by the owners of the road. Instead of having either the states or the federal government prohibit "speeding" or drunk driving, such laws will be determined by the owners of the road and recognized by the private courts as part of contract law (if there is a private court that doesn't recognize the right of an owner to make the rules of the road he owns such a person is free to find a court that will recognize his property right; one such court is bound to exist).

Section 19: States have a right to draft their own Constitutions. Much like the United State's 10th Amendment, we recognize the authority of the states to draft their own laws and challenge the authority of this Constitution. The only role that the Federal government has in telling states how to draft their own Constitution is in not having a state draft a law which forbids secession. No state may prohibit individual secession. Likewise, no state may require people who leave their state to be bound by the laws of their state (just like the people who leave Libertopia aren't bound by the laws of Libertopia), though the common law and typical international law does recognize the right of certain human rights which people may still be punished for violating even if they leave the state or country they were living in. We support the basic human rights, such as the right to life, liberty, due process, and property.

Section 20: It should be noted that this Constitution sets up the rules of Libertopia as well as mentioning some functions which no government agency can control. Those who don't want to be bound by the laws of Libertopia are free to secede. They don't have to leave their home and once they secede, as long as they keep their mitts to themselves, they are not subject to any of the laws of the Constitution, and the only positive obligation the following Constitution requires is jury duty.

The Costs of Coase

"Coase, get your cattle off my land." –Walter Block

Kip Viscusi, et al, mention the Coasian theorem as a supposedly free-market approach to deal with externalities. The Coasian theorem looks at wealth maximization in determining reciprocity. According to Coase, the assignment of property rights is irrelevant since however property rights are assigned, the property will go to the party who values the property the most (measured in their willingness to pay the most). According to Coase, the problem is not one of externalities but transaction costs. If the transaction costs are low, then both parties will bargain to an efficient outcome regardless of the initial allocation of property.

The example the authors use of Coasian bargaining addresses an example in which a farmer's cattle (Farmer A) strays onto another farmer's field (Farmer B) and damages his crops. According to Coase, it is irrelevant who has the property right. If farmer A has the right to let his cattle stray onto someone else's property or farmer B has the right to not have his crops damaged by another doesn't matter since if transaction costs are low, it is in the interest of both parties to bargain and the person who is willing to pay the most has the right. If farmer A has the right to let his cattle stray on farm B, then farm B will pay farmer A to build a fence if the damage of farm B's crop exceeds the cost of building a fence. If farmer B has the right to not have cattle stray on his property, then farmer A will pay to build the fence if the cost of building the fence is cheaper than the damage done to the crop. It doesn't matter who has the property right since either way the fence will be built; it's just a question of who pays to build it. Or in the words of Ronald Coase, *"such an agreement would not affect the allocation of resources but would merely alter the distribution of income and wealth as between the cattle-raiser and the farmer."* (Coase 1960, 5).

Coase acknowledged that bargaining isn't always possible since not all cases of externalities have low transaction costs (in the case of bilateral monopolies and free-riders who create a holdout problem making bargaining difficult). When transaction costs are high and bargaining isn't possible, the court should rule in favor of the party that is more economically efficient (i.e., increases social utility).

What is important about Coasian bargaining is to make sure that the person who pays the compensation isn't the person who necessarily damages the property but the person who can pay at the least cost. The example Coase gives is of a train that throws sparks that damage the property of farms. The question Coase asks is if the railroad should be liable for damages.

For instance, in Case 1: The farmer has the property right to not be damaged by sparks. Damage by fires amount to $200. A spark arrester costs $100. And the worth of goods that the railroad transports is $150. According to Coase, since the damage is greater for the farmer, the farmer has the property right and the efficient outcome is to have the railroad pay for a spark arrester or not to throw sparks.

In Case 2: This time, the value of the goods on the railroad is $400. The railroad has the right to throw sparks and the farmer has to either pay the railroad up to $200 to get him to stop throwing sparks or pay for a spark prevention device. In both cases, it is the railroad causing the damage to the farmer, yet in one case, the railroad is liable for the destruction he causes, and in the other one, he is not. According to Coase, *"With these figures it is clear that it is better...the railway should not be liable for the damage it cause, thus enabling it to operate profitably...By altering the figures, it could be shown that there are other cases in which it would be desirable that the railway should be liable for the damage it causes. It is enough for my purpose to show that, from an economic point of view, a situation in which there is 'uncompensated damage done to surrounding woods by sparks from railway engine' is not necessarily undesirable."* (Coase 1960, 34).

Gary North points out that according to Coase, "*a civil court has the obligation to allocate damages between the farmer and the railroad in its quest to maximize the public's social value. Each party damages the other, and the courts must allocate this damage. In Coase's legal world, the farmer's refusal to allow the railroad company to set fire to his crops is seen as imposing economic damage on the railroad company—damage which may be greater, in terms of reduced social utility, than the damage imposed on the farmer by the engine that spews out sparks.*" (North 2002, 79). Such a view justifies violating property rights under the vague excuse of "minimizing social costs."

For Coase, the justification for a particular set of rights is that they maximize wealth, which is why Coase criticizes Pigou by looking at property damage being determined by whoever caused the damage. For Coase, there is no one person who caused the damage. All actions involve harming one person at the expense of another. As Coase points out, "*We are dealing with the problem of a reciprocal nature. To avoid the harm to B we inflict harm on A. The real question that has to be decided is should A be allowed to harm B or should B be allowed to harm A?...In the case of the cattle and the crops, it is true that there would be no crop damage without the cattle. It is equally true that there would be no crop damage without the crops.*" (Coase 1960, 2 and 15).

What Coase is saying is that there is no such thing as one person damaging another person's property but rather in all externalities it is the fault of both parties. It may be true that the farmer's cattle destroyed the crops, but if there were no crops to destroy then the cattle wouldn't damage them, therefore, both parties are to blame. Economist Walter Block offered a perfect response to such nonsense: "*If I punch Coase in the nose, without provocation or mitigating circumstances under the old 'unsophisticated' legal dispensation, I could go to jail for assault and battery since I aggressed against him...it would be an open and shut case. Now consider what would occur under the Chicago school's legal dispensation. Here,...it is no longer clear that I aggressed against him. It is equally possible that he aggressed me by sticking his nose out at my onrushing fist."* (Block 2001, 4).

Another problem of Coase's theory is that you can't add people's utilities together. All costs (including transaction costs) are determined by the subjective values of each individual. Since each person's utility differs from everyone else, costs can't be added together. There is no way of knowing that the gain of the railroad is greater than the loss of the farmer's crops. People value their property beyond just monetary costs, but include psychic utilities as well. Since you can't add people's costs together, the idea of 'social costs' is meaningless. Coasian bargaining is viewed as a way to try to deal with externalities. Viscusi mentions that while the result will be the same irrespective of how property rights are assigned, he mentions that this might not be equitable. While the result in terms of who pays for the fence might be the same whether the crop owner or the cattle owner pays, it makes a great deal of importance to them who pays. According to natural law, a person is responsible for the damage they cause to another, while in the Coasian world it may sometimes be the responsibility of the victim to pay the aggressor in order to cease and desist or to pay for resources to compensate the aggressor for any destruction of property he caused. Coasian bargaining is inefficient and inequitable since it gives free reign for firms to damage the property of others if the firm is able to convince the courts that he did so in order to maximize social utility, since the gains from destroying property is worth more than the loss of property he destroyed. Without a principle of property rights, no one's property is safe. Instead of trying to defend the victim, Coase obscures who owns what. If it doesn't matter how property rights are determined then why does it matter if they are violated? Without understanding that a person owns himself and what he produces, how could one argue that pollution is something that should be regulated? The problem with negative externalities is that they harm another person or their property. The reason that pollution is bad is because it violates a person's property. Without this understanding, any talk of efficiency is vague and incoherent.

References

1) Viscusi, Kip, Joseph Harrington, and John Vernon. *Economics of Regulation and Antitrust*, 4th edition. MIT Press. 2005 pp. 745-787.
2) Coase, Ronald H. "The Problem of Social Cost." *Journal of Law and Economics Vol. 3.* University of Virginia, 1960, pp. 1-44.
3) Block, Walter. "O.J's Defense: A Reductio Ad Absurdum of the Economics of Ronald Coase and Richard Posner." Worcester: MA. College of the Holy Cross, 2001, pp. 1-20.
4) North, Gary. "Undermining Property Rights: Coase and Becker." *Journal of Libertarian Studies, Vol. 16.* Ludwig Von Mises Institute, (Fall 2002), pp. 75-100

The Economics of Bureaucracy

Daniel Rothschild

Coasian Bargaining, Property Rights, and The State

Abstract: The real purpose behind Ronald Coase's article, *"The Problem of Social Cost"* is to point out that government intervention as a solution to supposed market imperfections are not costless. Since government interventions can perhaps lead to greater costs than the problem the intervention is trying to correct, instead of assuming that government can fix the situation, it is instead necessary to apply the laws of economics to the real world and determine when government intervention is warranted and when a market solution is preferable. The problem with judging the real world in terms of assigning property rights based on maximizing social benefits and minimizing social costs is that it makes various assumptions that are not actually applicable to the real world. Coase views costs and benefits in the aggregate, assumes perfect information where the costs and benefits are known, ignores that property rights are defined and that initial allocation does matter, and believes that government rules are sometimes capable of maximizing value and wealth even though government rules are themselves not alienable property subject to economic calculation. Coase may consider it important to use economics to explain the real world, but then doing so involves looking at value as subjective and the world as existing in non-equilibrium, something Coase does not believe.

For Coase, the Coasian theorem assumes that agents attempt to maximize wealth. According to Coase, the assignment of property rights is irrelevant because however property rights are assigned, the property will go to the party who values the property the most (measured in willingness to pay). According to Coase, the problem is not one of externalities, but of transaction costs. If the transaction costs are zero, then both parties will bargain to an efficient outcome regardless of the initial allocation of property.

Coase acknowledged that bargaining isn't always possible since not all cases of externalities have low transaction costs (in the case of bilateral monopolies and free-riders who create a holdout problem, making bargaining difficult). When transaction costs are high and bargaining isn't possible, the court should rule in favor of the party who is more economically efficient (i.e., increases social utility).

Coase acknowledged that the theorem is an unrealistic depiction of the real world since in the real world there are positive transaction costs. The purpose of the Coase Theorem was not to depict reality as it exists, but to criticize Pigou, who believed that government taxing whoever causes the negative externality doesn't lead to problems of its own. Pigou acted as if there were no coordination problems and that the government knows both who is causing the negative externality and the amount of the damage caused by the negative externality in order to make sure the tax is neither too lenient nor too punitive. Coase developed the Coase theorem in order to both disprove Pigou and show how the problem is not one of externalities but of transaction costs, but also that economic theory should be based on the real world as it exists, and not be relegated to unrealistic blackboard armchair economics. As Coase states, *"Realism in our assumptions is needed if our theories are ever to help us understand why the system works in the way that it does. Realism in assumptions forces us to analyze the world that exists, not some imaginary world that does not."* (Coase 1982, 7)

According to Coase, the real lesson of his article, "The Problem of Social Cost," is comparative institutional analysis where in the real world of positive transaction costs, the goal should be to maximize wealth and output and that the appropriate rule is one that is done on a case-by-case basis where sometimes those who cause the damage should be liable and other times should not be, where in certain cases, the optimal choice is government regulation to deal with the externality or a market solution. According to Coase, *"It is all a question of weighing up the gains that would accrue from eliminating these harmful effects [i.e., externalities] against the gains that accrue from allowing them to continue."* (Coase 1960, 26) The problem, however, is that in the real world of positive transaction costs, there is no way to engage in a cost-benefit analysis of which rules are preferable. Unlike an open traditional market, the rules and the offices which enforce and define the property rights structure are not saleable property, subject to Coasian bargaining, market prices, and profit and loss.

Critique 1: Coase Assumes That How Property Rights Are Allocated and What Is Considered Property Doesn't Matter

In the real world of positive transaction costs where it's not possible for the person who values the property the most to bargain in order to obtain the property right, the court should give the property right to whomever maximizes social wealth and minimizes social costs. Or in Coase's words, *"The best outcome for the system as a whole [is] maximizing the value of total production (and in this sense I am Pigovian)"* (Coase 1990, 27).

Coase's view that the tools of economics should be used to analyze the real world and engage in comparative institutional (or property rights) analysis is admirable. Coase's view that judging whether government should change the rules, intervene, or support a market solution based on a case-by-case basis with the goal being maximizing aggregate value and minimizing social costs is confused, muddled thinking. The concept of aggregate value is a meaningless concept since value is based on subjective preferences. As Cordato makes clear, "*Costs and benefits are intrapersonally perceived. There is no interpersonal scale upon which they can be unified and ranked and therefore cannot be interpersonally aggregated. There is no economically meaningful way to talk about costs and benefits to society, apart from the individuals who experience them. Yet all social cost benefit analysis, by definition, makes this abstraction*" (Cordato 1998, 279).

Not only is the concept of social cost unclear, but so is Coase's views on property rights. While Coase acknowledges that different delimitations of property rights result in different allocations of wealth, and that "*one arrangement of rights may bring about a greater value of production than any other*" (Coase 1960, 16), Coase fails to provide a clear definition or theory concerning how property rights are defined. Coase's view on property rights is often at odds with how legal scholars have historically defined property rights. According to Coase, "*The rights of a land-owner are not unlimited...We may speak of a person owning land and using it as a factor or production but what the land-owner in fact possesses is the right to carry out a circumscribed list of action*" (Coase 1960, 44). Coase views property rights as a bundle of rights and as a right to use a resource for a certain purpose, such as maximizing social benefits and minimizing social costs, instead of viewing property rights as in rem claims against the whole world.

The in rem definition of property, where a person has a right to use their property as the individual wishes and that other persons have a negative right to not mess with their stuff leads to a type of security where the person knows his property will not be taken from him, and if so, that there is recourse against those who violate his property. Defining property rights as a right to a thing that no one may take from you without your consent influences people's future behavior because it makes your property rights more secure. Knowing that one has a right to use their property, not just so long as they use their property in the way the judges approve, but throughout time expands people's time horizons and allows them to make investments in the future.

According to such scholars as Adam Smith, William Blackstone, and Jeremy Bentham, by establishing a right to resources that holds against the entire world provides a security that people will be able to reap what they have sown (Merrill and Smith 2001, 361). For such scholars, the primary basis for property rights is to provide a sense of security against a range of interfering forces in society at large. In contrast to the Coasians (and much of law and economics today), where the primary purpose of the courts is to allocate property rights to whomever the courts feel uses the property in the way where the total value of production is maximized.

As Merrill and Smith explain, if property rights are determined based on whoever reduces social costs, such a rule incurs such costs and knowledge that no person is capable of fulfilling. If property rights are simply defined as the right to exclude others from using one's property, this rule allows the owner of the property to control, plan, and invest with a minimum of information costs to others, since people do not generally need to consult lists of use-conflict resolutions when they approach a property they do not own. Instead they know, unless otherwise stated, that the bright-line rules of trespass apply (Merrill and Smith 2001, 389). However, if property rights were defined based on using a resource in a way that maximizes social benefits, this would incur great information costs where each person has to know in advance how the court is likely to rule in order to avoid liability. As Merrill and Smith state, "*Each dutyholder would either incur great costs in informing herself, or would be forced to violate property rights wholesale, defeating the benefits of security, investment, and planning these rights were meant to secure*" (Merrill and Smith 2001, 387).

Critique 2: The Coasian Theorem Fails to Take Account of the Institutions Under Which Coasian Bargaining Takes Place

According to Douglas Allen, there are zero transaction costs (theoretically) when property rights are perfect. In the example of the farmer and the rancher, if the rancher is the one with the legal liability right, both his economic property right and his legal right are perfect. If the state or anyone else violates his property right without just compensation, that means that the rancher's property right is not perfect, and hence transaction costs are not zero (Allen 2014, 384). In order for there to be zero transaction costs, one's property rights must be perfect, which means that one's legal rights to use one's property must be perfect as well. If one can violate others' property and not be forced to compensate them, then transaction costs are not zero. As Allen states, *"either the rancher perfectly owns the right and must be compensated when it is removed, or he does not completely own it, and loses when it is taken away. Wealth only changes in this latter case where transaction costs are positive and the 'Coase Theorem' does not Apply"* (Allen 2014, 384). This naturally begs the question: how does one determine who has the legal right? How does one determine whether the legal right is valid or not? How does one determine the most efficient outcome? This requires that property rights do exist and can be clearly defined.

Yet the property rights institutions that enforce, protect, and define property rights are not themselves an alienable property subject to the Coase theorem. Therefore, the Coase Theorem fails to define the institutions upon which it is dependent as the offices that comprise and influence the institution do not represent alienable property. There is no way to know, using Coasian bargaining, if the property rights definition is the one that is most "socially optimal" since the owners of offices do not receive feedback comparable to profit and loss that occurs in a competitive market. If for Coase, wealth maximization is what determines whether the property right is efficient and that the legal institutions should give the property right to whomever reduces social costs the most, how is this possible when the legal institutions and the rules, definitions, and allocations are not subject to wealth maximization? Factions, politicians, and interest groups can influence the rules and office holders and these rules that are adopted may stem out of maximizing power for the rulers and the beliefs and values of those who prescribe the rules, and such beliefs need not be based on increasing overall wealth.

Control over the rules and process needed to generate them do not represent saleable property. Different initial allocation of control of the rules – allocation of the offices that influence them – can lead to divergent outcomes. Therefore, the concept of efficiency loses its meaning as a result of a lack of market prices which are absent under government institutions. The initial allocation of resources does matter when it comes to those that define and enforce the rules. Different holders of offices, particularly when an array of office holders comprise a faction, can promote different institutional trajectories. Certain transformations produce rules which lead to greater protection of property rights, whereas other transformations may lead to property rights being determined as a result of those with political clout and not as a result of free-bargaining individuals.

Instead of being measured in monetary terms, one possible Coasian alternative could be measuring in terms of votes, where those who value a certain candidate for political office are willing to buy the votes of those who do not value their votes as much as the amount they are willing to sell them for. One problem with using votes as a proxy for market prices is that rules and policies that are created under democratic governments are different from products sold on the market. A consumer is able to compare marginal units on one good with marginal units of another and is able to compare one alternative option with another. Goods in the market exist simultaneously along with other goods, but as DeCanio (2014) points out, the rules and policies that would be implemented don't occur alongside other alternative rules, but rather one hypothetical rule is exclusively produced (or chosen) in place of another hypothetical rule. Unlike the market for cars, where a person can compare driving a Ford with other cars, in politics with its winner take all system, there is no counterfactual. One can't compare President Trump alongside President Clinton and see which is preferable, but only can compare choosing what they imagine a Trump presidency would look like over what they imagine a Clinton presidency would look like.

Because the rules which are created determine the property rights structure under which property rights are defined and enforced, and because they influence how secure or tenuous property rights are, the initial allocation of the seats which define and enforce property rights matter. Present rules which create greater intervention in the economy impact and influence the future rules which may exist. Therefore, the initial allocation of the offices and seats of the governing institutions do matter in terms of creating divergent paths and shocks. The social conditions that exist differ depending on the rules which exist. Present rules create and influence future rules, so rules are path dependent. Factions can take over institutions and influence the rules, so the rules are constantly changing. Therefore, one can't make expectations about the future, making price discovery difficult.

Chris Coyne, Peter Leeson, and Boettke (hereafter CLB) have tried to explain what determines the success of rule of law and why it is respected and enforced in some areas but not in others. Borrowing a phrase from Ludwig von Mises, they have argued that the regression theorem determines the stickiness of institutions. Which institutions will stick and be successful depends on the institutions, norms, and culture of the previous time period. Or in their words, *"The regression theorem maintains that the stickiness, and therefore likely success, of any proposed institutional change is a function of that institution's status in relationship to indigenous agents in the previous time period"* (Boettke, Coyne, & Leeson 2008, 331).

CLB argues that there are three different types of institutions: those imposed by a domestic government, those imposed by a foreign government, and those that emerge spontaneously as a result of individuals' actions, but are not formally designed (Boettke, Coyne, & Leeson 2008, 335). The institutions that are the stickiest emerge spontaneously. If a foreign or domestic government enforces rules that already subscribe to the endogenous institutions, they are successful, while those that try to impose their legislation from top-down are not. CLB mention that the reason that reconstruction in Japan and West Germany succeeded was because both German and Japanese culture had a positive view of trade, market exchange, and democracy. In contrast, the reconstruction in Bosnia failed because the political climate and the climate of private individuals were not aligned. In Bosnia, there were numerous conflicting political interests, and when democracy was trying to be imported from above, there was no effort to get people's interests to coincide. Different political institutions within the nation-state had different, and often conflicting, constitutions. The timing of the elections was rushed before there was grassroots support. (Boettke, Coyne, & Leeson 2008, 349).

Calcagno, Hefner, and Dan point out that Neoclassical economists fail to understand the importance of economic calculation, and are more concerned with establishing equilibrium prices and macrostability. The Neoclassicals fail to understand that the macro economy is never in a state of equilibrium and that prices can only exist where there are private property rights. The Austrians understand that the real world, which Coase says he's concerned with, is in a state of non-equilibrium and change and that what is needed in order to have a successful market economy are institutions where private property rights are respected. Such institutions cannot be planned, but emerge spontaneously (Calcagno, Hefner, and Dan 2006, 42).

As CLB mention above, successful institutions cannot be imposed from above. Institutions which are successful in one society may not be successful in another. Social norms and values change slowly, whereas it's possible for a legal rule to change overnight. The acceptance of the legal system and the enforcement of laws depend on their acceptance and legitimacy by the masses in society. As Roland explains, *"Institutions generally form a system in the sense that each institution in the system is complemented by others, achieving a certain systemic consistency. Replacing one institution by another can in some cases dangerously disrupt this systemic consistency. Piecemeal institutional change in some directions is made impossible when there are strong complementarities among institutions"* (Roland 2004, 8).

While it may be possible to identify which societies are better off than others, it is often hard to figure out the reason why and the main causal link. Are predatory institutions a result of excessive regulations put in place by corrupt bureaucrats to extract bribes? Are they a result of inadequate separations of power within the government? Are such predatory institutions the result of differences in culture? (Roland 2004, 9). Likewise institutions are often not exogenous but themselves the product of other institutions and previous rules. For example, is it the social norms and culture which determine the legal rules which are adopted, or is it the other way around? Do legal rules influence and lead to changes in social norms? Since ceteris paribus is impossible when comparing differences among societies, it is often hard to figure out with certainty which way the causal effect runs.

Fernandez and Rodrik (1991) point out that the reason governments so often fail to adopt policies which economists consider to be more efficient is because there is a bias towards the status quo as a result of uncertainty. When people are unsure of who is going to gain from the new reform and who is going to lose, more people are likely to support the status quo if the winners cannot be identified beforehand. Even if the people against the new reforms would have supported it after the fact, if they are unsure who the winners and losers are going to be, they are less likely to take the risk that the new reform will make them better off, and so there is a bias towards the status quo.

3. The difference between the market and the government is that the market has a price mechanism to determine profit and loss, whereas the government is more reliant on ideas

As Mark Pennington (2004) points out, it is not the case that people in the market are aware of the results of all their actions and those in government are not. Rather, both those in the market and those in government lack perfect knowledge. The main difference, however, is that government top-down intervention is centrally planned, where legislatures are unable to discover the errors that their central planning creates. Pennington mentions that the competitive market process acts as an inter-subjective discovery procedure, where contradictory ideas are constantly tested against one another. Entrepreneurs don't start from the position of knowing which goods to produce, how to produce them, in what quantities, and at what price to produce them, but acquire such knowledge over time. Likewise, consumers do not start from the position of knowing what they want, but are constantly changing their preferences in light of changing offers which are continually presented by competing entrepreneurs (Pennington 2004, 218). A discovery process is created through competition, where profit and loss spread information about which courses of action are more (or less) successful. It is profit and loss which signal indicators of which actions are valued by the people whom they interact with. The market has a mechanism to deal with radical uncertainty: revealing that information to firms that their actions generated a profit and were successful at satisfying the consumer. Without profit and loss, and private ownership over the means of production, there is no way for market participants to improve the lives of those they interact with or know that the course of action they took was the right one.

The government, by contrast, does not operate on profit and loss, and therefore there is no mechanism in place which signals to those in government that their intervention created the desired result. Since government lacks the signal that acts as a knowledge surrogate, there is no way to know whether the course of action the interveners took was the right one. Since entrepreneurs have residual claimancy, they are able to transfer ownership to those who believe that are able to make a better use of the property than the current owner and in a sense engage in Coasian bargaining in order to obtain the property right to prove it. As Martin states, *"Transferable ownership [i.e. private property] allows those who believe they know a better use for durable production goods to make a tender offer, with residual claimancy providing a bulwark against cheap talk"* (Martin 2010, 234). Since government bureaus and the offices that define and enforce property rights lack residual claimancy, those in government who feel they can do a better job than the existing bureaus cannot buy the property from its current owner since government bureaus are not alienable property (Martin 2010, 225).

Wagner and Yazigi (2014) distinguish between experience goods and credence goods. Experience goods are goods that the consumer is not able to determine the quality of until after the good is purchased. In order to assure buyers that the quality of an experience is good, many sellers provide assurances such as money-back guarantees or brand-names in order to increase consumer trust and satisfaction. Credence goods on the other hand are goods where the consumer can never really be assured of the quality of the good (Wagner and Yazigi 2014, 11). Since the quality of credence goods can never be ascertained, the providers of such goods rely more on rhetoric—or ideas—as Martin (2010) calls it, since credence goods (or politics) rely more on convincing people that their ideas are good since government has loose feedback. Since the market has a tight feedback mechanism, where the quality of the goods can be proven in the form of profit and loss, the market (or experience goods) doesn't need to rely on cheap talk in order to garner support, but uses market signals and the price mechanism instead.

According to Wagner and Yazigi, political "goods" are a type of credence "good" because their quality cannot be ascertained even after the election. For example, Obama's stimulus package was a supposedly high quality good that resulted in reduced unemployment. Though unemployment rates increased after the stimulus package, the stimulus was not credited among its supporters as causing more unemployment. Rather, they claim that unemployment was going to increase anyway and if not for the stimulus package the unemployment rate would have been even worse (Wagner and Yazigi 2014, 12). Since political goods lack convincing counterfactuals, there is no feedback mechanism—such as profit and loss—to demonstrate which laws or candidate is the more wealth-maximizing, and so political decision-making relies on ideas instead, and these ideas are based on different value systems, such as possibly the normative values of the judge who renders the verdict.

Unlike government regulatory bodies, which lack both the technical and local knowledge and a pricing mechanism in order to determine whether such regulation passes the market test, for-profit competitors have a strong incentive to reveal the shadiness of other firms. Regulatory bodies are more likely to be captured by the industry and be susceptible to bribes. As Klein (1998, 548) points out, those in the market for assurance in order to signal their trustworthiness to others have an incentive to broadcast not only evidence of their trustworthiness, but also evidence of their competitors' lack of trustworthiness. They do so by making rival claims in their advertising, promotions, and marketing (Klein 1998, 548). As Klein states, "*Of the 65 advertising claims resolved by the Better Business Bureau's National Advertising Division in 1992, almost all of which dealt with the truth or accuracy of advertising claims, 47 were brought by competitors*" (Klein 1992, 548). Such safety assurance can only come about through a process of discovery, competition, trial, and error that depends on the local knowledge and circumstances of time and place. As Wildavsky points out, "*Safety results from a process of discovery. Attempting to short-circuit this competitive, evolutionary, trial and error process by wishing the end—safety—without providing the means—decentralized search—is bound to be self-defeating"* (Wildavsky 1988, 228).

4. Coase views knowledge as given, and not discoverable and dispersed

What is important about Coasian bargaining is to make sure that the person who pays compensation isn't the person who necessarily damages the property but the person who can pay at the least cost. The example Coase gives is of a train that throws a spark that damages the property of farms. The question Coase asks is whether the railroad should be liable for damages. For instance, in Case 1: The farmer has the property right to not be damaged by sparks. Damage by fires amount to $200. A spark arrester costs $100. And the worth of goods that the railroad transports is $150. According to Coase, since the damage is greater for the farmer, the farmer has the property right and the efficient outcome is to have the railroad pay for a spark arrester or not to throw sparks. In Case 2: This time, the value of the goods on the railroad is $400. The railroad has the right to throw sparks and the farmer has to either pay the railroad up to $200 to get him to stop throwing sparks or pay for a smoke prevention device. In both cases, it is the railroad causing the damage to the farmer, but in one case, the railroad is liable for the destruction he causes and in the other one he is not. According to Coase, *"With these figures it is clear that it is better...the railway should not be liable for the damage it cause, thus enabling it to operate profitably...By altering the figures, it could be shown that there are other cases in which it would be desirable that the railway should be liable for the damage it causes. It is enough for my purpose to show that, from an economic point of view, a situation in which there is 'uncompensated damage done to surrounding woods by sparks from railway engine' is not necessarily undesirable."* (Coase 1960, 34).

In Coase's above example of the farmer versus the railroad, Coase assumes the cost and benefits are given. The amount of damage by the railroad is provided, and so is the worth of the goods transported. All the judge has to do is compare the different given costs and see which one is greater. Ignoring for a moment that people have psychic costs and benefits and the amount of damage done according to the owner of the property is worth more than the monetary amount, the Coasian judge still fails to maximize the total value of production. If the goal is to maximize the total value of output, this implies considering third party effects that the rule the judge prescribes has. Since it is impossible for any fallible human to know the effects a ruling has, the judge is simply using his normative judgment about who is the least cost avoider. A case that allows uncompensated damage can lead to effects and influences on third parties. A rule which awards the property right to those who cause the damage can encourage others to cause more damage in the future with the belief that doing so will go unpunished as long as one is able to convince the judge that the benefit of him doing so is greater than the costs of violating someone else's property.

People have different preferences and spending patterns. If the goal is to maximize the total value of production, then the initial allocation of property rights does matter since the initial allocation of how property rights are assigned does affect the total value of production. One individual spends his income in a different way than another individual. Given that people are not simply wealth-maximizing robots, but have free will and choice, each individual has different spending patterns that in turn influences which businesses are successful and which are not. Suppose for example that there is a case where in order to ship goods worth $300, the railroad destroys the $100 window of a baker. The Coasian judge determines that the railroad is not liable for damages. It may take time before the baker is able to fix his window and because of this, his ability to sell his products decreases. Perhaps it takes two days to fix the window and overnight people steal $1,000 worth of damage as a result of the broken window failing to protect his store adequately. Or suppose the baker loses business worth more than the $300 the railroad ships since people do not want to shop in a windowless store and instead shop at the baker's competitor. In such a case, the Coasian judge ruled incorrectly since it turns out that more production was lost as a result of the broken window than the amount of the goods the railroad ships. Since we live in a world with time, these effects may not be visible at the time of such a ruling and therefore the judge fails to consider them. Since Coase is interested in maximizing the total value of production, it is necessary to take into account the long-term effects that the ruling may result in and not simply those short-term effects that are immediately visible.

5. Conclusion

While it may be important to make sure the laws of economics explain the real world, doing so requires rejecting many of the assumptions of Coasian bargaining in the real world of positive transaction costs. Since the offices which define property rights are themselves not alienable and subject to economic calculation, the concepts of economic efficiency and maximizing wealth are incoherent. The only way the rules concerning property rights can maximize wealth is if the rules themselves are produced for profit. Since the government lacks economic calculation, there is no way to know if the laws which define and enforce property rights maximize wealth since they are not subject to the market test.

Coase views the world in terms of equilibrium and ignores that the initial allocation of property rights does matter in terms of increasing overall wealth. If humans live in a static world of equilibrium, then perhaps the initial allocation of property rights doesn't matter in terms of affecting total output, but that's because total output is already given under such unrealistic conditions. As Coyne and Leeson (2004) have pointed out, entrepreneurship can either be productive or unproductive and that depends on the institutional structure and legal system that is in place. In a society where the legal system is corrupt or encourages rent-seeking, or the laws defining property rights don't match the norms of the society, then entrepreneurship is more likely to result in unproductive activity. This means that how property rights are defined does matter. It isn't enough to simply define property rights without knowing if how they are defined is in a way that encourages productivity.

According to Coase, *"To start our analysis with a situation approximating that which actually exists, to examine the effects of a proposed policy change and to attempt to decide whether the new situation would be, in total, better or worse than the original one. In this way, conclusions for policy would have some relevance to the actual situation"* (Coase 1960, 43). The reply to such a statement is better or worse according to whom and how does one measure or know what the total effect is? If better or worse is defined as whether a proposed policy change leads to more productivity than the situation beforehand, under how long a time span is Coase talking about? Since the policy changes are credence goods which are not produced for profit, how does one prove that the policy change is the causal factor in whether productivity increases? Perhaps productivity increases after the policy change, but would have increased even more so if not for the new rule. People to this day are still arguing whether the New Deal prolonged or shortened the Great Depression.

Rapaczynski (1996) mentions that protections of property rights are dependent on self-enforcing mechanisms which develop as part of the market process, and not by government fiat. Government defining property rights is not sufficient since people can't rely on the courts every time a dispute happens, (or the courts themselves might be corrupt and not trusted by many business firms) but instead have to rely on the confidence of those they do business with. The market provides assurance and reputational mechanisms to make sure property rights are respected and to develop trust to ensure a successful business. McChesney (1990) mentions that the government defining property rights of Indian lands actually weakened property rights protection for the Indians and allowed "the whites" to take over Indian lands. Government bureaucrats worked as an interest group to have the government define the property rights for Indian reservations since bureaucrats obtained a bigger budget by "privatizing" Indian lands (McChesney 1990, 326). Since the rules for privatization were not produced for profit, the rules ended up making the Indian landowners worse off and their property less secure since the rules concerning privatization according to the courts went against the Indian norms for allocating land ownership. While Coase acknowledged that government often has an incentive to define property rights in a way that benefits them, if this is the case then Coase ought to provide a theory in his paper on "The Problem of Social Cost" for what incentives are in place to reduce the likelihood of government defining property rights in a way that allocates property to themselves or their cronies; yet Coase fails to do so.

Viewing value as not subjective but objectively given implies that the judge knows how property rights should be decided since information is not dispersed. Even assuming benevolence and that the judge isn't influenced by special interests, his own views which might differ from the economist's are not based on maximizing social wealth since this information is not provided to the judge. The judge can look at current prices from different conflicting parties, but current prices are past data that don't reveal future prices. If Coase is interested in maximizing overall wealth assumes taking the future into account. Knowing whether a current policy or implementing a new one will provide a greater total benefit is something no judge is capable of knowing.

References

1) Allen, Douglas W. "The Coase theorem: coherent, logical, and not disproved." *Journal of Institutional Economics* 11.02 (2015): 379-390.
2) Boettke, Peter J., Christopher J. Coyne, and Peter T. Leeson. "Institutional stickiness and the new development economics." *American journal of economics and sociology* 67.2 (2008): 331-358.
3) Calcagno, Peter T., Frank Hefner, and Marius Dan. "Restructuring before privatization—putting the cart before the horse: A case study of the steel industry in Romania." *Quarterly Journal of Austrian Economics* 9.1 (2006): 27-45.
4) Coase, Ronald Harry. "The problem of social cost." *The Journal of Law and Economics* 56.4 (2013): 837-877.
5) Coase, Ronald H. *How Should Economists Choose?* G. Warren Nutter Lecture in Political Economy. Washington, dc : The American Enterprise Institute for Public Policy Research, 1982.
6) Coase, Ronald Harry. "The nature of the firm." *Essential Readings in Economics.* Macmillan Education UK, 1995. 37-54.
7) Cordato, Roy E. "Subjective value, time passage, and the economics of harmful effects." *Hamline L. Rev.* 12 (1988): 229.
8) Coyne, Christopher J., and Peter T. Leeson. "The plight of underdeveloped countries." *Cato J.* 24 (2004): 235.
9) DeCanio, Samuel. "Democracy, the market, and the logic of social choice." *American Journal of Political Science* 58.3 (2014): 637-652.
10) Fernandez, Raquel, and Dani Rodrik. "Resistance to reform: Status quo bias in the presence of individual-specific uncertainty." *The American economic review* (1991): 1146-1155.
11) Klein, Daniel B. "Quality-and-Safety Assurance: How Voluntary Social Processes Remedy Their Own

Shortcomings." *The Independent Review* 2.4 (1998): 537–555.

12) Martin, Adam. "Emergent politics and the power of ideas." *Studies in Emergent Order* 3 (2010): 212–245.

13) Medema, Steven G. "Economics and institutions." *Revue économique* 65.2 (2014): 243–261.

14) Merrill, Thomas W., and Henry E. Smith. "What happened to property in law and economics?." *The Yale Law Journal* 111.2 (2001): 357–398.

15) McChesney, Fred S. "Government as definer of property rights: Indian lands, ethnic externalities, and bureaucratic budgets." *The Journal of Legal Studies* 19.2 (1990): 297–335.

16) Rapaczynski, Andrzej. "The roles of the state and the market in establishing property rights." *The Journal of Economic Perspectives* 10.2 (1996): 87–103.

17) Roland, Gerard. "Understanding institutional change: Fast-moving and slow-moving institutions." *Studies in Comparative International Development (SCID)* 38.4 (2004): 109–131.

18) Pennington, Mark. "Citizen participation, the-knowledge problem-and urban land use planning: An Austrian perspective on institutional choice." *The Review of Austrian Economics* 17.2 (2004): 213–231.

19) Wagner, Richard E., and Deema Yazigi. "Form vs. substance in selection through competition: elections, markets, and political economy." *Public Choice* 159.3-4 (2014): 503–514.

20) Wildavsky, Aaron B. *Searching for safety*. Vol. 10. Transaction publishers, 1988.

Daniel Rothschild

Imitation is the Sincerest Form of Flattery:
A Critical Analysis of *Against Intellectual Monopoly*

Against Intellectual Monopoly by Boldrin and Levine ("B&L") makes the case that intellectual property does not promote innovation or lead to greater economic growth, by highlighting numerous examples from industries in which innovation increased without patent or copyright protection. The authors also argue that companies only try to obtain an intellectual monopoly after the well runs dry as a way to sit on their laurels and profit from past inventions by prohibiting competition. Therefore, patents and copyrights do not stimulate new inventions but instead reward past inventions.

The purpose of property rights is to reduce conflicts and to encourage production based on the premise that there would not be sufficient incentive to produce if others could free-ride off of the production of others. Intellectual property is different from owning something physical, such as a dog, in that, someone lending you his dog means he no longer has the dog, whereas sharing an idea with someone else does not mean the owner no longer has the idea. Similarly, the issue of whether an idea can be stolen is also important to the authors' argument. Stealing someone's physical property results in deprivation, where the thief deprives the owner of his product by redistributing it to himself. "Stealing" someone's idea, however, doesn't deprive the owner of his idea, rather instead of exclusive use, someone else has it as well. If theft is taking your property without consent, then by making a copy of your property, I didn't take anything from you; you still have it.

Boldrin and Levine discuss the "double-edged sword" of intellectual monopoly (B&L 2008: 11). The tradeoff inherent in intellectual monopoly is that if producers are rewarded a temporary government monopoly for innovations, this may encourage innovation. On the other hand, the existence of patents and copyrights increases the costs of creating a good, thereby lowering the amount of new entries into the field. The goal of a patent is to encourage new innovation by allowing the inventor to limit competition. This makes individual consumers worse off, but society better off since there will be greater investment in innovations. There is a trade-off between having newer innovations at higher prices or having more affordable redundant goods. Unfortunately, as the authors point out, intellectual monopoly encourages firms to create more patents – but not necessarily more products.

Boldrin and Levine discuss the pornography industry to demonstrate that weak enforcement of copyright yields greater production. Porn lacks the legislative protection of copyrights because it is met with moral opprobrium. Inarguably, the porn industry churns out more videos and at a cheaper cost than Hollywood. Furthermore, *"online pornographers are usually the first to exploit new technologies--from video-streaming and fee-based subscriptions to pop-up ads and electronic billing"* (B&L 2008: 41).

Then there is the issue of whether an idea has economic value. If I build a car, it has value, since people are able to drive to work faster than if they had to ride on a horse. But having the idea of a car and not producing it has no value since people's lives hasn't changed. It's the car that has value, not the idea of a car. Or, if I say to Professor Hummel that I didn't write a great critical review but had an idea that I did, it's likely he wouldn't accept such a response and reward me for my idea.

Boldrin and Levine provide empirical evidence showing that plenty of innovations and inventions existed without patent or copyright protection. Open-source software doesn't have patent protections, yet this is a thriving market. Linux is an operating system without patent protection and has 25% of the market share (B&L 2008: 20). The open source web server Apache has 68% of the market, while web servers that aren't open source and have patent protection, such as Microsoft and the Sun have significantly fewer customers. Microsoft has 31% and Sun has only 3% of the market (B&L 2008: 21). In fact, Apache's market share is increasing.

These examples highlight that patents and copyrights often have very little (if any) effect on encouraging innovations and that there were more innovations in areas with no intellectual monopoly than the opposite. A reason for the exponential growth of Silicon Valley is because California, as opposed to Massachusetts (home of Route 128), doesn't enforce trade-secrets, where past employees can't reveal information to the competitors they now work for. The problem with trade secret laws is that they don't take advantage of spillover effects. As Boldrin and Levine point out, *"large advances are generally built out of many small innovations. The process of innovation is greatly enhanced when innovators share information, enabling other innovators to bootstrap off of their advances. Because under competition all competitors can imitate, and so benefit from the innovation of everyone else, the incentive to share information is strong."* (B&L 2008: 155).

Boldrine and Levine mention the benefit of collaborative advantage that firms get by sharing information. Collaborative advantage is where, by sharing information, the inventor increases the odds of having competitors make improvements on his invention, thereby making the inventor better off by being able to sell a better product at a reduced cost. An example of collaborative advantage is the Cornish steam power engine that was not patented and ended up being improved by competitors.

Another important area the authors tackle is the pharmaceutical industry. Several points are made. The first is that countries in which there are no patent protections actually end up controlling a larger share of the world's drug market than countries that do. While the U.S, U.K. and France have patent protection, Switzerland and Germany (up until 1877) didn't have patent protection for their products. In 1862, British firms controlled about 50% of the world market and France had 40%. By 1873, German companies had 50% of the market and the French and British each had 13%-17% of the market (B&L 2008: 247). Even though there were patent protections for British companies to produce chemical products, most of the market share was dominated by countries that didn't have patent protection. Lack of patent protection didn't prevent German companies from innovating. In fact, the chemical industry of the U.S. was so underdeveloped that during WWI, the U.S. was forced to import dyes from Germany.

In addition to not suffering economic consequences, countries that had no (or weak) patent protection had the most innovation, while the countries with patent protection innovated less. 20 of the 46 top selling drugs were created without patents, and out of the 26 remaining, 4 were discovered by accident and then patented (B&L 2008: 259-260).

Advocates of intellectual property argue that drug patents are necessary because the industry has large fixed costs. It takes a lot of resources and investment to find and create new drugs. They claim that without patent protection, drug companies wouldn't want to take the risk of losing all the money they spent on research. However, the authors argue that advertising and marketing will allow better capture of revenue than patenting and that drug research should be subsidized. Furthermore, there are numerous fields which require large fixed costs and whose products can be easily replicated, yet this doesn't discourage people from entering the market and competing. The existence of Dunkin Donuts didn't discourage the creation of Starbucks.

Boldrin and Levine mention that the cost of clinical trials amounts to 80% or more of the total cost of developing a new drug (B&L 2008: 268). According to Boldrin and Levine, clinical trials could be considered a public good because the costs of paying for the clinical trials are high, but the cost of sending out the information to others is low. This means that once the health risks of a new drug are discovered, competitors can benefit from this information without having to pay for the clinical trial themselves. Boldrin and Levine recommend that a government agency like the (National Institutes of Health) NIH pays for clinical trials, diminishing the need for patents.

Since Boldrin and Levine mention how patents are a form of rent-seeking, it's strange that they would advocate government spending as a way to solve the problem in the pharmaceutical industry. The problem with having the government pay for research is that it would lead to rent-seeking. The type of research could be determined by those with political clout. According to Richard Gilbert, *"It is not clear that any agency, even one as informed as the NIH, would have opportunities and demand possessed by private firms and eliciting this information from private firms would be difficult"* (Gilbert 2009: 425).

Because a lot of the justifications for intellectual property laws are based on protecting the work of the creator, Boldrin and Levine mention ways that creators can protect their creation without patents and copyrights. The first-mover advantage is where the early bird gets the worm. They argue that being the first to come up with a new invention gives the firm an advantage that those who copy his ideas lack. The first person to sell a product gets all the customers until competitors enter the market. It can take years until copycats are able to make and sell the product. Boldrin and Levine point out that many people who buy from a company are loyal and remain lifelong customers of that company. They point out that 80% of book sales occur within the first three months of publication (B&L 2008: 158). According to Hugh, Moore, and Snyder, after a patent expires and generic drugs are available, the original drug is still able to charge a monopoly price and dominate 20% of the market (B&L 2008: 266).

While it's harder to copy someone else's innovations and come up with the technology to compete, making copies of a book is much easier and cheaper to do. A copy of a book is almost identical to the original, so wouldn't there need to be a copyright to ensure that writers have incentives to create written works? The answer is that for a publisher to copy every book on the market is expensive. A person who just made copies of random books without figuring out the demand for them first would quickly go out of business. Copying books costs money, so the way to have these resources be profitable is to only copy books that are in high demand. If the incentive is to copy books that are already in high demand, this means that the books themselves are popular and have sold millions of copies already, thus reimbursing the author before copies are made. While this argument is pretty sound, it's not universally true. If a book has advance praise and popularity well before the book is released, then copiers don't have to wait until the books have sold millions of copies to know that they will have a market for copies of the books. Are people who make copies of the 3-7th books of the *Harry Potter* series really taking a risk by copying the book? Boldrin and Levine never address this possibility.

While patents are a clear violation of property rights, it's highly unlikely that two people come up with the same book. Boldrin and Levine weaken their arguments by putting copyrights within the same camp as patents and not making a distinction. If their argument against intellectual property is that intellectual property discourages innovation and competition, how does this apply to copyrighted works? Patents often cover broad ideas, while copyrights protect people from making a carbon copy of an already existing product. For instance, Boldrin and Levine mention how in 1895 George Selden came up with a "road engine" and without actually creating it, merely patented the idea and then used the patent to collect 1.25% royalties from all automobiles sold in the U.S., which he later sold for greater profits (B&L 2008: 93). Selden's "submarine patent" didn't add any production to the economy. Selden never created any automobiles and even if he did, someone else would have come up with the same idea in the near future. On the other hand, if J.K. Rowling never created Harry Potter, it's highly unlikely that someone else would have. No monkey has ever actually churned out Hamlet.

John de Laubenfels mentions that forbidding copyrights undermines private contracts. Unlike patents, which don't involve a contract that stipulates that the author will only sell the work on the condition that the buyer won't make copies of it and distribute them, copyrights involve contracts between the buyer and seller. People engaged in a transaction have a right to sell their product under certain conditions and if the other party agrees and then breaks the contract they have committed fraud and should be penalized. Patents on the other hand don't involve contracts between a seller and buyer.

While it's important to distinguish between patents and copyrights, de Laubenfels' critique is flawed for a few reasons. One, as Boldrin and Levine point out, copyrights prevent both the copier from selling copies and the buyer from buying them. The author of the original work only had a contract with the person who bought his work (the copier) and not any potential customers of the person he sold his creative work to. Therefore, if copyright law should exist at all, only the person who bought the work from the original owner is bound by contract. Likewise, it should be legal to "pirate" software, and download music and movies since in such a case there was no contract. Someone who illegally downloads movies from the internet never had an agreement with the movie studio that he wouldn't download. Just because someone tells you not to do something doesn't mean you're required to listen.

In conclusion, *Against Intellectual Monopoly* challenges the view that intellectual property is needed to encourage innovation. Increased patents and copyrights don't lead to an increase in goods and services, but are lobbied by special interest groups as a way to profit off of past inventions instead of having to come up with new ones. Instead of big companies using resources going to production, they are devoted to lawsuits and lobbying to extend patent life and discourage new entries for fear of a lawsuit. Boldrin and Levine are right to call intellectual property for what it is—a monopoly. A monopoly is where competition is restricted due to state-sanctioned protection. The way to have more useful goods and services isn't to restrict entry but to allow competition to flourish. As Frederick Bastiat understood, *"competition is merely the absence of oppression."* For the sake of both respecting private property and productive economic growth, let's end this oppression.

References

1) <u>Boldrin</u>, Michele and <u>David K. Levine</u>. *Against Intellectual Monopoly*." Cambridge: Cambridge University Press, 2008, pp. 1-325.
2) Gilbert, Richard. "A World without Intellectual Property?" *Journal of Economic Literature*, 2011, pp. 421-432.
3) <u>deLaubenfels</u>, John. "Dissecting Boldrin and Levine: An Alternate View of Intellectual Property," 2009. Found at: <u>http://www.strike-the-root.com/91/delaubenfels/delauben</u> <u>fels1.html</u>

The Economics of Bureaucracy

Don't Steal; The Government Hates Competition:

The Problem with Civil Asset Forfeiture

Daniel Y. Rothschild
George Mason University

Walter E. Block
Loyola University, New Orleans

Republished with permission from The Journal of Private Enterprise & Edward Stringham

---

Abstract

Governments originally meant for civil asset forfeiture laws to take the profit out of crime and show that crime literally does not pay. Since governments keep the seized assets for themselves, however, these laws lead to perverse incentives. Instead of police using resources to fight crime that has actual victims, police go after drug buyers to find assets to seize to increase the police budget. This paper attempts to show that police are ordinary, rational people who attempt to maximize their welfare. Police unions lobby to block regulations that limit forfeiture laws; seized assets and drug arrests have gone up while drug usage has not. Instead of trying to reduce crime, the police become the criminals by taking honest people's belongings. This paper also shows the effect of forfeiture on drug prices and how law enforcement has no incentive to reduce arrests for victimless crimes.

JEL Codes: H0, H1, H10
Keywords: theft, government, competition, civil asset forfeiture

"Vices are those acts by which a man harms himself or his property. Crimes are those acts by which one man harms the person or property of another. Vices are simply the errors that a man makes in his search after his own happiness. Unlike crimes, they imply no malice toward others, and no interference with their persons or property. In vices, the very essence of crime—that is, the design to injure the person or property of another—is wanting. It is a maxim of the law that there can be no crime without a criminal intent; that is, without the intent to invade the person or property of another. But no one ever practices a vice with any such criminal intent. He practices his vice for his own happiness solely, and not from any malice toward others. Unless this clear distinction between vices and crimes is made and recognized by the laws, there can be on earth no such thing as an individual right, liberty, or property; no such things as the right of one man to the control of his own person and property, and the corresponding and coequal rights of another man to the control of his own person and property. For a government to declare a vice to be a crime, and to punish it as such, is an attempt to falsify the very nature of things. It is as absurd as it would be to declare truth to be falsehood, or falsehood truth."

—Lysander Spooner (from his 1875 article, "Vices are not Crimes")

I. Introduction
There are two types of forfeiture laws. Criminal forfeiture requires a person charged with committing a crime to give up property used to commit the crime or obtained in the act. It is known as an in personam crime, which means that the person is considered guilty of breaking the law[1]. Civil forfeitures, by contrast, are in rem, which means that the object itself is considered guilty of committing a crime[2].

---

[1] In personam is Latin for "against a person."
[2] In rem is Latin for "against a thing."

Criminal forfeitures require higher standards of proof than civil forfeitures, since only humans have rights and objects do not (Warchol and Johnson 1996, p. 62)[3].

The Constitution applies to people only, which means that for criminal forfeiture, people receive constitutional protections; they cannot have their assets seized until and unless they are actually found guilty of a law violation. Criminal forfeiture requires that a person who is accused of committing a crime has a right to a trial. He or she must be found guilty beyond a reasonable doubt. It is up to the prosecutor to prove guilt, and only after the accused is proven guilty may the assets that were involved in the criminal act be seized. Civil forfeiture, on the other hand, does not require such "high standards" (Kelly and Kole 2013, p. 3). This type of confiscation requires only probable cause for one's property to be seized, and the usual legal presumptions are all turned around: the accused has to prove innocence instead of the prosecutor proving guilt[4]. Since civil forfeiture requires less evidence and offers fewer protections than criminal forfeiture, the former is more vulnerable to abuse than the latter. This paper focuses on civil forfeiture and its consequences.

In section 2, we look at the history of this legal practice. Section 3 discusses modern developments. In section 4, we analyze equitable sharing; in section 5, conflicts of interest. We conclude in section 6.

II. History

The legal practice of civil forfeiture arose in medieval times[5]. It was based on the superstitious notion that it was the object itself that had committed the crime, and the object was forfeited to the king. For example, the crown

---

[3] It is a sorry state of affairs that we feel obligated to cite such a claim.

[4] The protections of civil forfeiture differ from state to state (Worrall 2008, p. 9).

[5] Note, we say "legal," not licit nor appropriate.

could seize an object that resulted in someone's death in order to pay for the victim's funeral (Williams, Holcomb, and Kovandzic 2010, p. 10). The common idea that guns cause crime and not the person pulling the trigger is a contemporary example of such a superstitious belief. Civil forfeiture is based on the notion that inanimate items have minds of their own. Taken to its logical conclusion, the only murderers who should be incarcerated are those who killed victims with their own bodies; if a man used a knife or a gun to murder someone, the murderer should be set free, while the gun and knife are imprisoned[6].

Civil forfeiture is an old concept that existed in the common law (Doyle 2008, p. 2). However, its employment in the United States is based on the British Navigation Acts (BNA) of the mid-seventeenth century, which required that imports and exports to and from Britain be carried on ships bearing that nation's flag. If the acts were violated, then "the ships or the cargo on board could be seized and forfeited to the crown regardless of the guilt or innocence of the owner" (Williams, Holcomb, and Kovandzic 2010, p. 10). The justifications for such laws were to ensure protection against pirates seizing cargo and to collect customs duties. The government justified taking ownership because it was impossible to seek justice against property owners, since they were overseas[7]. Former US Supreme Court justice Joseph Story defended this practice, stating that the "vessel which commits the aggression is treated as the offender, as the guilty instrument or thing to which forfeiture attaches, without any reference whatsoever to the character or conduct of the owner...from the necessity of the case, as the only adequate means of suppressing the offense or wrong, or insuring an indemnity to the injured party" (Williams, Holcomb, and Kovandzic 2010, p. 10). The justification for adopting this

---

[6] It is difficult to come up with a sillier reductio ad absurdum, and yet, as we shall see later, this practice also occurs in the modern era.

[7] Well, justice at least in the interpretation of the authors of the BNA.

practice was that it was going to be used in a limited manner, in cases where it was almost impossible to locate the victim.

Throughout most of US history, the use of civil asset forfeiture was a rarity. It was utilized during the War between the States of 1861 and during alcohol prohibition (Pimentel 2012, p. 10). Unfortunately, civil asset forfeiture has been common practice since 1984 (Kelly and Kole 2013, p. 4).

III. The Modern Era

In order to take the profit out of drug money, the Comprehensive Drug Abuse Prevention and Control Act of 1970 was passed (Blumenson and Nilsen 1998, p. 44). The funds the police seized were deposited in the Treasury's general fund. The money would go to the federal government and be distributed among different departments to fund various public services. The Comprehensive Crime Control Act of 1984 allowed state and local law enforcement to seize assets used for illegal activity. Before the Comprehensive Crime Control Act, seized assets were considered property of the government and were placed in a general fund, but subsequently the proceeds were taken over by the police agencies themselves (Chi 2002, p. 1639).

The goal of the Comprehensive Crime Control Act was to give police incentives to pursue drug crimes by allowing them to keep the seized assets. As Joseph W. Dean of the North Carolina Department of Crime Control and Public Safety bluntly admitted, "The United States Attorney General . . . requires that all shared property be used by the transfer for law enforcement purposes. The conflict between state and federal law would prevent the federal government from adopting seizures by state and local agencies . . . If local dand state law enforcement agencies cannot share, the assets will in all likelihood not be seized and forfeited. Thus no one wins but the drug trafficker . . . If this financial sharing stops, we will kill the goose that laid the golden egg" (Benson, Rasmussen, and Sollars

1995, p. 31).

Another goal of the Comprehensive Crime Act was to add resources to the police budget. This would supposedly have two beneficial effects: (1) to take the profit out of crime by seizing drug money and (2) to increase the police budget, making more funds available to fight crime. Funding the police budget in this way also reduces the taxes needed to finance the constabulary, saving the taxpayer money.

The Comprehensive Crime Act allows "equitable" sharing, which permits state and local law enforcement agencies to seize assets and transfer them to their federal counterparts; the latter then share some of the proceeds with the former. This so-called "equitable" sharing only applies when the "object" itself is accused of violating a federal law (United States Department of Justice 2009, p. 6).

Not all states have enacted such laws, and some have stricter ones than others. For example, in Delaware, the government only needs to show probable cause to seize someone's assets. It is up to the owner to prove his innocence. If he or she cannot, then law enforcement keeps 100 percent of the assets seized (Williams, Holcomb, and Kovandzic 2010, p. 52)[8]. Maine has stricter requirements: it employs the preponderance of evidence test. But the accused still has to prove innocence. Unlike Delaware, all forfeiture proceeds go into Maine's general fund instead of the Department of Justice Assets Forfeiture Fund, thus providing less of a conflict of interest for police (Williams, Holcomb, and Kovandzic 2010, p. 63).

IV. Equitable Sharing
Under equitable sharing, the seized assets are subject to the federal government standard of forfeiture law: the

---

[8] Thus, the legal maxim "innocent until proven guilty" no longer applies.

preponderance of evidence. As well, up to 80 percent[9] of the property taken goes to the Equitable sharing allows the state and local police in jurisdictions with greater limits to override them by being subject to the federal government's lower legal requirements.

If police are interested in maximizing their wealth, the evidence should show that equitable sharing is done more in states that have higher standards of proof and that allow police to keep fewer of the seized assets than the federal government. Since the latter allows police to keep the seized property, there should be more equitable sharing in states that do not allow law enforcement to keep all of the seized assets[10]. This is exactly what the empirical results confirm. For example, as Williams, Holcomb, and Kovandzic (2010, p. 37) reveal: Results indicate law enforcement agencies in generous forfeiture states receive significantly lower equitable sharing payments from the Department of Justice. For example, each 25 percentage point decrease in the state profit motive (say, from 100 percent to 75 percent) boosts federal equitable sharing by $7,500 per year. This is for a law enforcement agency serving an average-sized population of 300,000. Thus ... law enforcement agencies in states with no profit motive will receive, on average, four times that amount—$30,000— compared to agencies in states where 100 percent of proceeds go to law enforcement. Put another way, 26 states permit law enforcement to use all civil forfeiture proceeds. If these states were to do away with the profit motive, they could expect law enforcement to turn more to equitable sharing, with the average-sized

---

[9] For another type of critique of this practice, one consistent with our analysis, see Epstein (1985)

[10] We make this claim with extreme trepidation. Were this an attempt to explain and understand business behavior in the private market, we would have no such compunctions. For in that arena, if a firm does not engage in profit-maximizing behavior, it tends to go bankrupt. There is no such mechanism at work in the statist sector of the economy.

agency taking in $30,000 more in equitable sharing proceeds.

Not only should we see greater equitable sharing in states where not all of the proceeds go to law enforcement, but there should also be more of this in states with higher standards of proof than the federal government. As Williams, Holcomb, and Kovandzic (2011, p. 280) show:

Per capita equitable sharing payments for agencies located in states where the burden in innocent owner defenses is on the government can be expected to increase by 3-cents [10*.001 + 10*1*(.002) = .03] for every 10 percent increase in state proceeds returned to law enforcement. On the other hand, a similar 10 percent increase can be expected to reduce per capita equitable sharing proceeds by 1- cent per person [10*.001 + 10*-1(.002) = 0.01] when the burden of proof standard is on the claimant. Simply put, for agencies expecting large returns on forfeiture activity, placing the burden of proof on the owner to establish his or her innocence equates to less reliance on federal forfeiture programs. . . . Specifically, in states where the owners are presumed innocent (i.e. the burden is on the government to establish an owner's guilt), raising the standard of proof by one unit has the net effect of increasing per capita equitable sharing payments by .057 cents per person[1*.030 + 1*1*(.027) = .057] as compared to only .003 cents per person [1*.030 + 1*-1*(.027) = .003] when the burden switches from the government to the owner.

The alleged justification for applying civil forfeiture to drugs is to take the profit out of this victimless crime[11]. Yet, instead of the police going after drug dealers, they pursue buyers. The police use a "reverse sting," where they pose as drug sellers. This is because our forces of "law and

---

[11] For the case in favor of legalizing narcotic drugs (not an urging of their use, a very different matter) see Block (1993, 1996); Block, Wingfield, and Whitehead (2003); Cussen and Block (2000); Friedman (1992); Szasz (1985, 1992); and Thornton (1991).

order" would rather have money than drugs. As Miller and Selva (1994, p. 252) explain, "The reverse sting is the preferred approach because agents can control and calculate the amount of money a deal will involve before they can commit time and resources."

What are the incentives for individual police officers to seize assets from innocent victims? As Steven L. Kessler, the former head of the Bronx District Attorney's forfeiture unit, points out, "The NYPD uses confusion about the code to take money from people who didn't do anything. There is a cash incentive for the NYPD to take the money—it goes to their pension, it can even be used to buy equipment, to throw parties. You see a nice car parked outside of a precinct? That's the result of civil forfeiture. Now it's theirs" (Rivlin Nadler 2014).

A case that shows the perverse incentives of civil asset forfeiture is that of Gerald Bryan. Police burst into his home and took $4,800, which they suspected of being drug money. Bryan is one of the few people who have fought back against a civil forfeiture lawsuit, and he got his money back. The money reimbursed to him came out of New York City's general fund instead of its police pension fund. Hence, even though Bryan got back the money that was wrongly seized from him, the taxpayers footed the bill. The police officer kept the money he improperly seized for his pension (Balko 2014).

Representative Henry Hyde wanted to reform forfeiture laws by making it harder for police to seize people's assets. Hyde sponsored the Civil Asset Forfeiture Reform Act of 2000 (CAFRA). The goal of this bill was to require higher standards before government employees could seize a person's property. CAFRA shifted the burden of proof from the accused to the prosecutor. Instead of just probable cause, Hyde's law required a preponderance of the evidence in order to take away assets, counsel for the accused, and the award of "attorney's fees to litigants who have substantially prevailed against the government in civil forfeiture proceedings" (Rulli 2001, p. 88).

While CAFRA's goal is to offer more protection against the accused, Hyde did not add provisions to eliminate equitable sharing from the bill because of political lobbying from the police bureaucracy. Law enforcement engaged in booty seeking by lobbying against any efforts that would reduce the amount of money they could keep from a seizure[12]. CAFRA also led to a substantial increase in forfeiture since it boosted the number of offenses subject to civil asset forfeiture at the federal level (Kelly and Kole 2013, pp. 6–7).

V. Conflicts of Interest
Because of police efforts, bills such as CAFRA have had no real effect in eliminating the conflict of interest that stems from keeping seized assets. This initiative still allows "the taint doctrine" (aka the relation-back doctrine), which says that any object that was used (or merely accused of being used) in a criminal act belongs to the government even if the actual owner of the property did not commit the act (Worrall 2004, p. 222). Consider in this regard Bennis v. Michigan, where Tina Bennis jointly owned a car with her husband. The police took the automobile since Mr. Bennis had sex with a prostitute in it. Even though Mr. Bennis is the one who committed the "crime," it doesn't matter: according to civil forfeiture, it is the object—the vehicle—that is "guilty," not the person (Chi 2002, p. 1642).

Mast, Benson, and Rasmussen (2000, p. 287) point out that police devote more resources to drug arrests than to other crimes. Since the men in blue are interested in padding their budgets, economic theory (Mises 1944; Niskanen 2007; Tullock 1987) suggests an increase in drug arrests relative to other types of crimes. When the Comprehensive Drug Abuse Prevention and Control Act of 1970 was passed,

---

[12] In the public choice literature, this is often called "rent-seeking." We refuse to employ this term for reasons given by Block (2000a, 2000b).

subsequent drug arrests per capita from 1970 through 1984 were relatively constant. But then came the Comprehensive Crime Control Act of 1984. After its passage, "drug arrests per 100,000 population rose by 72 percent" from 1984 through 1989 (Mast, Benson, and Rasmussen 2000, p. 287). According to the FBI (2012), the highest number of arrests is for drug abuse violations (estimated at 1,552,432 arrests in 2012 alone).

Civil forfeiture means that police resources are not being used in other areas. For every cop seizing assets, there is one fewer available to arrest real criminals for violent crimes. Victimless crime arrests lead to an increase in violent crimes in two main ways: given limited resources, there are fewer gendarmes available to stop violent crimes, and just as police attempt to maximize their utility, criminals do so as well (Becker 1974; Ehrlich 1972, 1973, 1974). One of the main reasons for arresting people is deterrence. Criminals are more apt to commit "crimes" when the odds of getting arrested are lower (Benson and Rasmussen 1998, p. 78). When police increase the amount of seizures and arrests in one field (drug dealing and selling), that field becomes less appealing. Raising the odds of punishment for drug offenses causes a substitution effect, as criminals move from drug crimes toward those for which they are less likely to be caught. This means there should be more violent crimes being committed[13]. As comedian George Carlin understood, having prisons in your neighborhood reduces crime since all the criminals are locked up and if some do escape, "What do you think they're gonna do? Hang around? Check real estate prices? Bull! They're . . . gone! That's the whole idea of breakin' out of prison: to get as far away as you possibly can" (Carlin 2002, pp. 110–11).

VI. Conclusion
Civil asset forfeiture law is both immoral and a failure. The

---

[13] Violent crimes—defined by the FBI (2012) as murder and nonnegligent manslaughter, forcible rape, robbery, and aggravated assault—have actual victims.

stated goal was to take the profit out of crime, but instead of going after dealers, most police efforts aim at buyers. According to Eric Sterling, the director of the Criminal Justice Policy Foundation, "Only 11 percent of drug offenders in federal prison are high-level traffickers, while more than 50 percent are low-level" (Blumenson and Nilsen 1998, p. 71). Further, as former San Jose, California, police chief Joseph McNamara points out, drug prohibition inflates the cost of drugs (since supply is artificially suppressed), which not only causes an increase in shady characters willing to take the risk of supplying drugs, but even causes some policeman to become drug gangsters. When the men in blue are not busy seizing money from innocent people (remember, it is supposedly the object, not the person, that is guilty), thousands of them are selling narcotics as a side job in order to get a bigger budget. One of the most famous examples is Lieutenant Colonel James C. Hiett, a twenty-four-year Army veteran whose wife shipped $700,000 worth of cocaine and heroin through the US Embassy in Bogota and sold it in the United States (McNamara 2011, p. 112).

Since police are able to obtain 80 percent of seized assets due to so-called equitable sharing, they have less incentive to take the profit out of crime, since for them, crime is profitable[14]. People's property is being taken away from them without a trial. Police seize their assets, trump up criminal charges, and agree to drop those charges if property is relinquished.

The gendarmes lobby to weaken any changes to the law that would decrease the amount of assets earmarked for their department. Instead of reducing crime, forfeiture increases crimes that have actual victims, since police resources are being directed toward victimless drug offenses instead. Violent crimes increase as the risk of being caught goes down.

---

[14] As Milton Friedman (1992) explained, "If you look at the drug war from a purely economic point of view, the role of the government is to protect the drug cartel. That's literally true."

The solution we propose is a radical one. Any alternatives and attempts at a compromise have been shown to fail. We suggest not   reform, but a repeal of forfeiture laws. Equitable sharing must be ended. Objects do not commit crimes: people do. Civil forfeiture has not taken the profit out of crime; rather, it places profit in crime and gives the real criminals—the police—legal immunity. Civil forfeiture reveals the hypocrisy of the state for all to see, and it is not a pretty sight.

References

Balko, Radley. 2014. "Gothamist on Asset Forfeiture Abuse at NYPD." Washington Post, January 15.

Becker, Gary S. 1974. Essays in the Economics of Crime and Punishment. New York: National Bureau of Economic Research.

Benson, Bruce L., and David W. Rasmussen. 1998. "Deterrence and Public Policy: Trade-Offs in the Allocation of Police Resources." In International Review of Law and Economics, 77–100. New York: Elsevier Science.

Benson, Bruce L., David W. Rasmussen, and David L. Sollars. 1995. "Police Bureaucracies, Their Incentives, and the War on Drugs." Public Choice, 83(½): 21–45.

Block, Walter. 1993. "Drug Prohibition: A Legal and Economic Analysis." Journal of Business Ethics, 12 (July), 689–700.

Block, Walter. 1996. "Drug Prohibition, Individual Virtue and Positive Economics." Review of Political Economy, 8(4): 433–36.

Block, Walter. 2000a. "Watch Your Language." Mises Daily, February 21. Block, Walter. 2000b. "Word Watch." Mises Daily, April 20.

Block, Walter E., Katherine Wingfield, and Roy Whitehead. 2003. "Re-Evaluating America's Failing Drug Control Laws: A Legal, Philosophical, and Economic Proposal." Oklahoma City Law Review, 28(1): 119–59.

Blumenson, Eric, and Eva Nilsen. 1998. "Policing for Profit: The Drug War's Hidden Economic Agenda." University of Chicago Law Review, 65: 35–114. Carlin, George. 2002. Napalm & Silly Putty. New York: Hyperion. Chi, Karis Ann-Yu. 2002. "Follow the Money: Getting to the Root of the Problem with Civil Asset Forfeiture in California." California Law Review, 90(5): 1635–73. Cussen, Meaghan, and Walter E. Block. 2000. "Legalize Drugs Now! An Analysis of the Benefits of Legalized Drugs." American Journal of Economics and Sociology, 59(3): 525–36.

Doyle, Charles. 2008. Crime and Forfeiture. Hauppauge, NY: Nova Science Publishers, 1–89.

Ehrlich, Isaac. 1972. "The Deterrent Effect of Criminal Law Enforcement." Journal of Legal Studies, 1(2): 259–76.
Ehrlich, Isaac. 1973. "Participation in Illegitimate Activities: A Theoretical and Empirical Investigation." Journal of Political Economy, 81(3): 521–65. Ehrlich, Isaac. 1974. "Participation in Illegitimate Activities: An Economic Analysis." In The Economics of Crime and Punishment, ed. Gary Becker and William Landes, 68–134. New York: Columbia University Press. Epstein, Richard A. 1985. Takings: Private Property and the Power of Eminent Domain. Cambridge, MA: Harvard University Press.
FBI. 2012. "Crime in the United States 2012."
Friedman, Milton. 1992. "The Drug War as a Socialist Enterprise." In Friedman & Szasz on Liberty and Drugs, ed. Arnold S. Trebach and Kevin B. Zeese. Washington, DC: Drug Policy Foundation.
Friedman, Milton, and Thomas Stephen Szasz. 1992. Friedman & Szasz on Liberty and Drugs: Essays on the Free Market and Prohibition. Arnold S. Trebach and Kevin B. Zeese, eds. Washington, DC: Drug Policy Foundation.
Kelly, Brian D., and Maureen A. Kole. 2013. "The Effects of Asset Forfeiture on Policing: A Panel Approach." Forthcoming in Economic Inquiry. December 30, 1–35.
Mast, Brent D., Bruce L. Benson, and David W. Rasmussen. 2000. "Entrepreneurial Police and Drug Enforcement Policy." Public Choice, 104(September): 285–308.
McNamara, Joseph D. 2011. "The Hidden Costs of America's War on Drugs." Journal of Private Enterprise, 26(2): 97–115.
Miller, J. Mitchell, and Lance H. Selva. 1994. "Drug Enforcement's Double-Edged Sword: An Assessment of Asset Forfeiture Programs." Justice Quarterly, 11(2): 245–67.
Mises, Ludwig von. 1944. Bureaucracy. New Haven, CT: Yale University Press. Niskanen, William A. (1971) 2007. Bureaucracy and Representative Government. Piscataway, NJ: Aldine Transaction.
Pimentel, David. 2012. "Forfeitures Revisited: Bringing Principle to Practice in Federal Court." Nevada Law Journal, 13(1): 3–59.

Rivlin-Nadler, Max. 2014. "How The NYPD's Use of Civil Forfeiture Robs Innocent New Yorkers." Gothamist, January 14.

Rulli, Louis S. 2001. "The Long Term Impact of CAFRA: Expanding Access to Counsel and Encouraging Greater Use of Criminal Forfeiture." Federal Sentencing Reporter, 14(2): 87–97.

Spooner, Lysander. (1875) 2010. "Vices Are Not Crimes: A Vindication of Moral Liberty." In The Shorter Works and Pamphlets of Lysander Spooner, vol. 2 (1862–1884). Indianapolis, IN: Liberty Fund.

Szasz, Thomas Stephen. 1985. Ceremonial Chemistry: The Ritual Persecution of Drugs, Addicts, and Pushers. Holmes Beach, FL: Learning Publications.

Szasz, Thomas Stephen. 1992. Our Right to Drugs: The Case For a Free Market. New York: Praeger.

Thornton, Mark. 1991. The Economics of Prohibition. Salt Lake City: University of Utah Press.

Tullock, Gordon. 1987. The Politics of Bureaucracy. Landham, MD: University Press of America.

US Department of Justice. 2009. Guide to Equitable Sharing for State and Local Law Enforcement Agencies, 1–47.

Warchol, Greg L., and Brian R. Johnson. 1996. "Guilty Property: A Quantitative Analysis of Civil Asset Forfeiture." American Journal of Criminal Justice, 21(1): 61–81.

Williams, Marian R., Jefferson E. Holcomb, and Tomislav V. Kovandzic. 2010. Policing for Profit: The Abuse of Civil Asset Forfeiture. Arlington, VA: Institute for Justice.

Williams, Marian R., Jefferson E. Holcomb, and Tomislav V. Kovandzic. 2011. "Civil Asset Forfeiture, Equitable Sharing, and Policing for Profit in the United States." Journal of Criminal Justice, 38(3): 273–85.

Worrall, John L. 2004. "The Civil Asset Forfeiture Reform Act of 2000: A Sheep in Wolf's Clothing?" Policing: An International Journal of Police Strategies & Management, 27(2): 220–40.

Worrall, John L. 2008. "Asset Forfeiture." Problem-Oriented Guides for Police Response Guides Series, No. 7. Albany, NY: Center for Problem-Oriented Policing.

Daniel Rothschild

Freeze, So I Can Take Your Stuff!

Abstract: This paper reports findings from my investigation of the effect of civil asset forfeiture on the state of California. I investigated the effect that civil asset forfeiture has on different cities in the State of California. The intention of this study was to build on Baicker and Jacobson's research by looking at the overall effects of the cities' budget to determine if civil forfeiture (and equitable sharing) leads to an increase in the amount of total funds for the city. My hypothesis is that the amount of money seized in an earlier year predicts the total budget of the subsequent year. This hypothesis was tested using a linear regression analysis. Since forfeiture goes to both police resources and the general fund, it was of interest to determine if there is a relationship between the amount of seized assets and cities' budgets. Based on publicly available data, the primary analysis, testing the relationship between civil forfeiture in 2009 and total city budgets in 2009-2010, was performed. A series of other analyses were performed to determine alternative explanations for the association between seizure and city budgets.

Introduction: There are two types of forfeiture laws, one that pertains to persons and one that pertains to objects. Criminal forfeiture refers to a situation in which a person is charged with, and is considered guilty of, committing a crime. Criminal forfeiture is known as an 'in personam' (Latin for "against a person") crime. Civil forfeiture is known as an 'in rem' (Latin for "against a thing") crime and refers to the circumstance in which an object is considered guilty of committing a crime. Criminal forfeitures require higher standards of proof than civil forfeitures because humans have rights while objects do not. The Constitution applies only to people. Therefore, under the circumstance of criminal forfeiture, persons have constitutional protections before having their assets seized. Criminal forfeitures also require the accused to be found guilty beyond a reasonable doubt. Thus, the accused has a right to a trial and the prosecutor must prove guilt prior to seizing any assets.

Civil forfeiture, on the other hand, only requires probable cause for one's property to be seized (although the protections of civil forfeiture differ from state to state). The accused has to prove his innocence instead of the prosecutor proving his guilt. Since civil forfeiture requires less evidence prior to seizure of property and fewer protections than criminal forfeiture, civil asset forfeiture is more vulnerable to abuse than criminal forfeiture.

<u>Background</u> -- Throughout most of United States history, use of civil asset forfeiture was a rarity. It was used during the Civil War and during (alcohol) Prohibition. The use of civil asset forfeiture has increased and has become a more common practice since 1984 (Moores 781: 2009). There are several contributors to the increased use of civil asset forfeiture.

In order to get tough on drugs and to take the profit out of drug trafficking, Congress passed the Comprehensive Drug Abuse Prevention and Control Act of 1970 (Blumenson and Nilsen 1998: 44). The funds that the police seized were deposited in the Treasury's General Fund where that money would go to the federal government and be distributed among different government departments to fund various government services. Then, the Comprehensive Crime Control Act of 1984 allowed state and local law enforcement to seize assets used for illegal activity and to have those assets go to the Department of Justice instead of being used in the general fund. Before the Comprehensive Crime Control Act, seized assets were considered property of the government and were put in a general fund, but now the proceeds the police collect are kept by the police agencies themselves.

The goal of the Comprehensive Crime Control Act was to give police incentives to pursue drug crimes by allowing them to keep a significant proportion of the seized assets.

Another goal of the 1984 Act was to add resources to the police budget. This had two beneficial effects: 1) Taking the profit out of crime by seizing drug money and 2) Increasing the police budget to have more funds available to fight crime with, which also reduces the taxes needed to fund the police.

The Comprehensive Crime Act of 1984 made a provision for equitable sharing. Equitable sharing allows state and local law enforcement to take assets they seize and transfer them to federal law enforcement agencies; the federal law enforcement agencies then share some of the seized assets with the state or local police. Equitable sharing only applies where the "object" is accused of violating a federal law. (United States Department of Justice 2009: 6).

Under equitable sharing, the seized assets are subject to the federal government standard of forfeiture law, which is the preponderance of evidence. Up to 80% of assets seized go to the Department of Justice fund (Worrall 2008: 8). Equitable sharing allows the local police in states with higher standards to seize a person's assets more easily, effectively overriding local laws in favor of more liberal government standards.

This paper looks at the relationship that forfeiture has on the budgets of various cities in California for the following year. Do cities with more forfeitures increase the funds that go to the local police or do they notice that since police have more seizures they have less of a need for more funds the next year? Or is there no relationship between forfeiture, the cities' total budget and the amount given to police?

Literature Review

The best (and most thorough) study on the effects of civil asset forfeiture is by Williams, Holcomb, and Kovandzic (2010), which looked at the effect of forfeiture on crime rates and the police budgets in all 50 states. Williams, Holcomb, and Kovandzic reviewed the requirements for seizing a person's assets (e.g. preponderance of the evidence and probable cause) to determine whether states with higher standards had more police seizing assets. Their study revealed that since the federal government's standard is weaker than many other states, the authors conclude that more equitable sharing is done in states with a higher standard of proof than the federal governments.

Benson and Rasmussen (1998) compared the crime rate of Florida before and after the war on drugs. They determined the arrests rate for Index I crimes (crimes that have victims) and non-Index I crimes ("victimless crimes") and demonstrated that forfeiture leads to police arresting people for non-Index I crimes. Mast, Benson, and David W. Rasmussen (2000) compare Index I crimes and police arrests and point out that forfeiture leads to an increase in Index I crime arrests since more police resources are devoted to non-Index I crimes. Since the odds of getting caught are lower for Index I crimes, criminals have a substitution effect by going into crimes where the chances of being caught are less likely.

Rulli (2001) compared civil asset forfeiture after CAFRA (The Civil Asset Forfeiture Reform Act of 2000) and showed that while CAFRA offers more protections for property owners before being able to seize a person's assets, not only is the protection weak but civil forfeiture has increased after CAFRA since there are now more "crimes" subject to forfeiture. Rulli also indicated that, after CAFRA, civil forfeiture leads to an increase in criminal forfeiture. This is because CAFRA provides the accused the right to an attorney so people are able to contest the charge. Bringing the case to trial leads to more convictions. Before CAFRA, the standards were lower and people were less willing to contest the charge (since they would have to pay for the lawyer themselves).

Kelly and Kole (2013) looked at panel data sets to see if police respond to civil asset forfeiture by using more resources devoted to seizing assets. Kelly and Kole demonstrated that there is some statistical support that police agencies change the pattern of policing as a result of forfeiture, but in economic terms these effects are very weak. Kelly and Kole used Law Enforcement Management and Administrative Statistics (LEMAS) data, which are derived from a questionnaire that asks police officers how much forfeiture they seize. They also look at FBI's Uniform Crime Reports (UCR) to see which areas the police are devoting their energies to in order to see if more resources are going to seizures. Kelly and Kole demonstrated that the conclusion that police are devoting more resources to go after seizing assets is over-exaggerated.

Baicker and Jacobson (2007) evaluated the relationship between local spending and police seizures and found that local governments offset police seizures by reducing the amount of funds they give to police the following year. Baicker and Jacobson also (2007: 2123) used data from the Drug Enforcement Administration's *System to Retrieve Information from Drug Evidence* (STRIDE) from the years 1977-1999. STRIDE records purchases and seizures of illegal drugs made by undercover DEA agents and informants. According to Baicker and Jacobson (2007:

2132): *"The effect of de facto sharing on log cocaine prices is small and imprecise. In contrast, forfeiture incentives are associated with a clear increase in the log price of heroin, the most commonly used illicit opiate: evaluated at the mean de facto sharing rate of 0.33, the coefficient of 4.14 implies an elasticity of heroin prices with respect to real sharing of 0.14."*

What the above literature implies is that there is some relationship between police behavior and civil asset forfeiture. Rulli concludes that the relationship is very weak and Baicker and Jacobson conclude that there is a negative relationship between police seizure and policing behavior in the sense that when the police get fewer funds as a result of forfeiture, they do a cost-benefit analysis to see if they make more money through seizure or through the bureau.

This paper reports findings from my investigation of the effect of civil asset forfeiture on the state of California. I investigated the effect civil asset forfeiture has on different cities in the State of California. The intention of this study was to build on Baicker and Jacobson's research by looking at the overall effects of the cities' budget to determine if civil forfeiture (and equitable sharing) leads to an increase in the amount of total funds for the city government. My hypothesis was that the amount of money seized in an earlier year predicts the total budget for the subsequent year. This hypothesis was tested using a linear regression analysis. Since forfeiture goes to both police resources and the general fund, it was of interest to determine if there is a relationship between the amount of seized assets and the city's budget. Based on publicly available data, the primary analysis testing the relationship between civil forfeiture in 2009 and total city budget in 2009-2010 was performed. A series of other analyses were performed to determine alternative explanations for the association between seizure and city budgets.

Data And Methodology

The majority of the data were obtained from the Rand

Corporation, while other data came from the Department of Justice Forfeiture Fund and the FBI. The Sources I found are listed in Table 1 below.

To calculate funds that go to the cities, I subtracted the equitable sharing (the amount of assets that go the police agencies) from the total amount of forfeiture seized, which is labeled 'NONPOLICESHARE' on the graph below.

In the first step of the analysis, I obtained descriptive statistics on the variables and then performed a simple correlation on the variables to determine the relationship among the variables.

Because population was significantly correlated with almost every other variable in the regression analysis, for each of the subsequent analyses, I adjusted for the population size, so as to better understand the relationships between the other variables. Population was therefore entered in the regression model as a control variable. The methodological approach to estimating the relationship between forfeiture in the previous year and budgets in the subsequent year was to construct a model using ordinary least squares as follows:

$$\text{TOTALFUNDS2010i} = \beta 0 + \beta 1\text{FORFEITURESi} + \beta 2\text{CITYPOPULATION2009i}$$
$$+\beta \text{DEV1} +\beta \text{DEV2} +u \ (1)$$

Where 'TOTALFUNDS2010i' is the dependent variable and refers to the amount of funds available to city i, the primary independent variables are Civil Asset Forfeitures collected in 2009 and City Population in 2009, and the β's are coefficients to be estimated and ui is an error term with the usual properties. A series of sequential analyses were based on a similar model.

RESULTS: Table 1 lists the variables used, their definitions, and the sources from which the data were gathered.

VARIABLE	DESCRIPTION	SOURCE
#POLICE2009	Number of police in 2009	UNIFORM CRIME REPORTS (From FBI)
FORFEITURES	Civil Asset Forfeitures: Fines, Forfeitures, Total Revenues 2009	RAND Corporation
CITYPOPULATION2009	Population 2009	RAND Corporation
CASHVALUE2009	Cash Value of what police seize through equitable sharing in 2009	Department of Justice Asset Forfeiture Program
SALEPROCEEDS2009	The amount of money the police make by selling the proceeds they seize.	Department of Justice Asset Forfeiture Program
EQUITABLESHARE2009	CASHVALUE2009+Sales SALEPROC2009 = TotalShare2009 (Equitable sharing). This is the total amount of forfeiture due to equitable sharing for 2009.	Department of Justice Asset Forfeiture Program
TOTALFUNDS20092010	The total city budget (amount of money the city gets) for 2008-2009	RAND Corporation
NONPOLICESHARE	Forfeitures – (minus) Equitable sharing for non-police agencies or moneys not available to police but transferred to other departments	RAND Corporation
POLICESHARE	Equitable share/ (divided by) forfeitures = percentage of forfeitures due to equitable sharing (this was determined by dividing the amount of equitable sharing over the amount of forfeitures).	RAND Corporation

Table 1. Variable Definitions and source

Table 2 provides summary descriptive statistics for the variables in Table 1.

Variable	Obs	Mean	Std. Dev.	Min	Max
City	0				
#POLICE2009	78	247.7	304.0	25	1749
FORFEITURES	80	$3,361,141	1.76E+07	4,644	1.55E+08
CITYPOPULATION2009	48	96,329	100,879	7,698	495,231
CASHVALUE2009	60	$231,648.4	383,949.2	0	1,667,798
SALEPROCEEDSS2009	60	$416,13.6	114,161.7	0	749,921
EQUITABLESHARE2009	60	$273,262.1	410,886.6	1,371	1,796,959
TOTALFUNDS20092010	80	$4.90E+07	6.31E+07	2415011	3.31E+08
NONPOLICESHARE	60	$392,6014	2.02E+07	-1678860	1.55E+08
POLICESHARE	60	$2.712143	11.26787	0.000802	86.455

Table 2: Summary Statistics

Seven OLS regressions were created in order to determine the impact that civil asset forfeiture has on police behavior and cities' budget. **Regression 1** determines whether total forfeiture in 2009 predicted total budget for the cities in 2010, controlling for population in 2009. **Regression 2** determines whether the number of police employed in 2009 predicts revenue from equitable sharing of forfeiture in 2009. **Regression 3** determines whether the number of police employed leads to an increase in civil asset forfeiture in 2009. **Regression 4** determines whether what is seized through forfeiture predicts equitable sharing, controlling for the number of police and population.

Regression 5 determined whether the number of police engaged in forfeiture is correlated with the amount of assets that go to the police agencies directly.

This regression was done by creating the variable POLICESHARE, which is the percentage of equitable sharing out of forfeitures. The variable FORFEITURES looks at the total value of seizures through forfeitures (of each city) and the variable TOTALSHARE2009 looks at the total amount of seized assets that go to the police agencies themselves, whereas the variable POLICESHARE is the percentage of forfeitures due to equitable sharing (this was determined by dividing the amount of equitable sharing over the amount of forfeitures). **Regression 6** determines if the amount of equitable sharing has on the total funds of the city budget for the following year.

Regression 7 looks at the amount of forfeiture that goes to non-police agencies (the variable NONPOLICESHARE) on the total city budget for the following year. This was done by creating the variable NONPOLICESHARE, which was determined by subtracting equitable sharing from the total forfeitures. Since equitable sharing is the amount of forfeitures that the police agencies keep, and FORFEITURES includes both equitable sharing and non-equitable sharing seizures, in order to find out the amount of seizures that go to non-police agencies, I subtracted the variable EQUITABLESHARE2009 (the total value of assets seized through equitable sharing) from the variable FORFEITURES (the total value of assets seized) in order to get the variable NONPOLICESHARE (the total value of assets seized that get transferred to other non-police government agencies).

Variables	#POLICE 2009	FORFEIT URES	CITY POPULAT ION 2009	CASH VALUE 2009	SALE PROCE EDS 2009	EQUITAB LESHARE 2009	TOTAL FUNDS 2009-20 10	NONPO LICESH ARE	POLICE SHARE
#POLICE 2009	1								
FORFEITURES	0.2807	1							
CITYPOPULATION 2009	0.7142	0.2769	1						
CASH VALUE 2009	0.6762	0.1038	0.4902	1					
SALE PROCEEDS 2009	0.0007	-0.0133	-0.056	0.0059	1				
EQUITABLE SHARE 2009	0.6393	0.0938	0.4452	0.9469	0.3271	1			
TOTAL FUNDS 2009-2010	0.2403	0.2779	0.235	0.092	-0.0086	0.0842	1		
NONPOLICE SHARE	0.1337	0.9739	0.1742	-0.1125	-0.0878	-0.1346	0.2574	1	
POLICE SHARE	-0.0554	-0.1467	-0.0176	0.0374	0.3488	0.1475	0.0161	-0.1796	1

Table 3: Correlation Matrix

As the correlation table (Table 3) shows, there is mostly a positive relationship between the number of police and the other variables, except for the # of police and the amount that police share there is a negative relationship. It appears that the greater the number of police there are, the less incentive there is to engage in equitable sharing since the benefits are more dispersed. For FORFEITURES, the relationship is mainly positive, though there is a negative relationship between FORFEITURES and POLICESHARES. Population of cities is mostly positively correlated, except for SALEPROCEEDSS2009 and POLICESHARE. CASHVALUE2009 is positively correlated for most categories, except for the amount of seized assets that go to non-police agencies; the same relationship is true when it comes to SALESPROCEEDSS2009. As predicted, there is a positive relationship between equitable sharing when the proceeds go to the police department but not when the proceeds get shared to other agencies. There is a positive relationship between TOTALFUNDS20092010 and the amount that goes to all departments.

Results

The regression data demonstrate a small relationship between how much forfeiture is seized and how many funds go to the cities. As Table 4 demonstrates, there is a correlation between how many assets are seized and how much funds the cities receive.

In regression 1, forfeitures are significant predictors of budget, even after controlling for population. Therefore, an increase in civil asset forfeiture leads to an increase in the government's coffers. This conclusion, however, may be premature because there are other variables, demonstrated below.

Regression 2 demonstrates a significant relationship between the amount of equitable sharing and the number of police officers. Thus, when police are able to keep the seized assets for themselves, there may be more incentive to have more police involved in seizing assets.

Regression 3 shows there is no relationship between the number of police and civil forfeitures. When considered in the context of the above analysis, it could be hypothesized that if most of the seized assets go to the police agencies instead of being shared among different departments, more police resources are being devoted to forfeiture. There is no relationship between forfeiture on its own, only when equitable sharing is being used.

The greater the number of police the greater the equitable sharing. Population size was not relevant. But there is no relationship between the number of forfeitures and the number of police. Therefore, if police get to keep the seized assets for themselves, they will seize more assets. However, as economic theory suggests, the total number of forfeitures isn't relevant to how many assets the police seize. When part of the forfeiture is handed over to the states, police don't increase the number of assets they seize. Therefore, without equitable sharing, there isn't enough incentive for police to increase the amount of resources they use being devoted to seizures. There is a weak correlation between the number of police and the number of seizures. Forfeiture has little (to no) effect on increasing the police budget.

As regressions 6 and 7 show, there is a strong relationship between the amount of forfeiture that goes to the police department themselves and the amount of forfeiture that goes to other departments. The amount of seized assets leads to an increase in the city's budget the following year. The more assets that are seized, the more funds the city has.

Regression 6 shows that the percentage of assets that goes to the police agencies (POLICESHARE) is significant at the 1% level but is not significant at the 5% and 10% level.

Regression 7 shows that the percentage of forfeiture that is given to non-police agencies is significant at the 1% and 5% level and that the total funds for 2009-2010 is statistically significant at the 1%, 5%, and 10% levels. This means that the total funds increase due to civil asset forfeiture as a result of equitable sharing, irrespective of where the funds go. Equitable sharing causes an increase in the cities' total budget, both when the police agencies get to keep the seized assets and when they have to share the assets with other government agencies.

Variables	Regression 1	Regression 2	Regression 3	Regression 4	Regression 5	Regression 6	Regression 7
Dependent Variables:	Model 1 TOTAL FUNDS 2009-2010	Model 2 EQUITABLES HARE2009	Model 3 FORFEITURE	Model 4 EQUITABLES HARE 2009	Model 5 POLICE-SHARE	Model 6 POLICE-SHARE	Model 7 TOTALFUNDS 2009-2010

CITYPOPULATION 2009	106.0 (92.3)	-0.095 (0.912)	2.77 (2.43)	-0.0362 (0.96)	5.9e-.06 (1.3-05)	5.4e-.06 (1.3e-05)	79.3 (101.7)
FORFEITURES	4.69*** (1.68)			-0.02 (0.001)			
#POLICE 2009		958.6*** (309.8)	985.5*** (755.7)	981.4*** (316.6)	-0.004 (0.006)	-0.004 (.0006)	
TOTALFUNDS 2009-2010						9.2e-09 (2.9e-08)	
POLICESHARE							5.04** (2.08)
Constant	2.627e+07*** (9.359e+06)	71,944 (54,595)	550,748 (336,462)	83,133 (59,646)	4.295 (2.885)	3.958* (2.233)	3.547e+07*** (1.205e+07)
Observations	48	36	47	36	36	36	36
R-squared	0.136	0.409	0.086	0.417	0.004	0.005	0.104

Robust standard errors in parentheses
*** p<0.01, ** p<0.05, * p<0.1
Table 4: Regression Results

The results of the analyses are as follows:

Regression 1 indicates that there is a significant relationship between total forfeiture in 2009 and total budget in 2009-2010 controlling for population, which is a variable that did not contribute significantly to the model. This supports the primary hypothesis that the amount of assets seized in one year predicts the budget in the following year.

In Regression 2, it can be seen that there is a significant relationship between the number of police in a given city and the amount of revenue that is received from equitable sharing. Regression 3 shows that there is no significant relationship between the number of police and the amount of forfeitures, but the overall model was significant $F(2,44=3.42, p=0.04)$. Regression 4 demonstrated that the number of police also predicts equitable sharing. Regression 5 demonstrates that there is no relationship between the percentage of assets that the police get to keep through equitable sharing and the amount of equitable sharing. Regression 6 shows that the percentage of assets that the police get to keep through equitable sharing is also not related to the total funds or number of police. However, Regression 7 shows that the percentage of assets that police get to keep through equitable sharing is a significant predictor of the subsequent year's budget.

Because the data on civil asset forfeiture is compiled by the FBI themselves, there may be some bias in the results as police departments have an incentive to underreport the amount of assets that they seize. Another limitation of this study is that while up to 80% of seized assets (due to equitable sharing) go to the police agencies themselves, the data does not reveal how much each cities' police department gets to keep from the equitable sharing of the assets. As shown in Table 4, I was able to calculate the percentage of assets seized due to equitable sharing and how much is seized without equitable sharing, but I was not able to figure out how much each city gets to keep due to equitable sharing. Therefore, the significance due to police behaviors due to equitable sharing is a rough estimate.

Another limitation on the study is that I determined the impact that forfeiture has on the police budget for the following year by using the increase in police employment as a proxy variable, with the understanding that police may have an increase in budget that is not reflected by the increase in the number of police employees.

For future research, if it's possible to calculate the exact percentage each city and state gets to keep due to equitable sharing, the effect of forfeiture on police behavior is likely to be more precise and the relationship more significant.

Conclusion

Baicker and Jacobson (2007) looked at local spending and police seizures and found that local governments offset police seizures by reducing the amount of funds they give to police the following year. According to my research, the opposite seems to be the case.

The difference between Baicker and Jacobson's data and my own is that they don't compare assets seized due to equitable sharing and assets seized without equitable sharing, whereas I make the distinction between assets seized by working with the federal government (equitable sharing) and assets seized by working on the local level only (non-equitable sharing). Baicker and Jacobson do take account of the fact that only a certain portion of the assets goes directly to the police agencies, but they don't specify if that's due to equitable sharing or not. Perhaps this accounts for the difference in our results.

As shown above, there is a strong relationship between the amount of property seized and the budget for the city the following year. While there is a strong relationship between the amount of seized assets and the total budget for the city (regardless of equitable sharing), the correlation between the number of police and the forfeiture seized only occurs when there is equitable sharing. The correlation that police increase the amount they seize and the number of police is strong when done via equitable sharing, but there is no relationship between the number of police and the amount they seize when seized without the local law enforcement working with the federal government.

When police seize assets, there is a strong correlation between the amount they seize and the total funds the cities get (whether due to equitable sharing or not). Without equitable sharing, fewer police resources are being used to seize assets.

If the government is interested in increasing the amount of civil asset forfeiture, it seems that equitable sharing provides a strong incentive for police to seize assets, but without equitable sharing, there is no strong incentive for police since the assets they seize get transferred to other departments. While a lack of equitable sharing creates less of a conflict of interest between police and residents, even when police don't engage in equitable sharing, the local budget still increases when forfeiture is being used. Therefore, cities have incentives to encourage the use of equitable sharing, as a way to increase their own budget.

The more police officers there are, the more equitable sharing there is. Increasing the number of police employees increases the amount of police resources being devoted to equitable sharing, but not the amount of forfeiture. Therefore, having more police doesn't mean that more resources are being devoted to seizing assets.

References

Baicker, Katherine and Mireille Jacobson. "Finders Keepers: Forfeiture Laws, Policing Incentives, and Local Budgets. *Journal of Public Economics*, Elsevier B.V., 2007, pp. 2113–2136.

Benson, Bruce L. and David W. Rasmussen. "Deterrence and Public Policy: Trade-Offs in the Allocation of Police Resources." *International Review of Law and Economics*, New York: Elsevier Science Inc., 1998, pp. 77–100.

Blumenson, Eric and Eva Nilsen. 1998. "Policing for Profit: The Drug War's Hidden Economic Agenda." *The University of Chicago Law Review*, Vol. 65, No., , pp. 35–114.

Guide to Equitable Sharing for State and Local Law Enforcement Agencies. U.S. Department of Justice, 2009, pp. 1–47.

Kelly, Brian D. and Maureen A. Kole. "The Effects of Asset Forfeiture on Policing: A Panel Approach." (December 2013), pp. 1–35.

Mast, Brent D., Bruce L. Benson, and David W. Rasmussen. "Entrepreneurial Police and Drug Enforcement Policy." *Public Choice*, Netherlands: Kluwer Academic Publishers, 2000, pp. 285–308.

Moores, Eric. 2009. "Reforming the Civil Asset Forfeiture Reform Act." *Arizona Law Review*, Vol. 51, pp. 777–803.

Rulli, Louis S. "The Long Term Impact of CAFRA: Expanding Access to Counsel and Encouraging Greater Use of Criminal Forfeiture." *Federal Sentencing Reporter*, Vol. 14, No. 2, Forfeiture: Recent Reform and Future Outlook, University of California Press: Vera Institute of Justice, (September/October 2001), pp. 87–97.

Williams, Marian R., Jefferson E. Holcomb, and Tomislav V. Kovandzic. *Policing for Profit: The Abuse of Civil Asset Forfeiture.* Institute for Justice. (March 2010) pp. 6–120.

Worrall, John L. 2008. "Problem-Oriented Guides for Police Response Guides Series

Guide No. 7: Asset Forfeiture." *Center for Problem-Oriented Policing*, The U.S. Department of Justice, pp. 1–62.

Daniel Rothschild

More (Government) Police, More Crime

Abstract: What do government police do and how does one measure whether what they are doing is beneficial (i.e. engage in a cost-benefit analysis, absent market competition, profit and loss, and a price mechanism). Unlike private defense, government (or public) police are in the business, not of defending people from criminals, but of enriching themselves and enlarging their bureau's budget and power. The following essay will conduct an economic analysis of state police, what their incentives are, how they operate, some measurement problems, why the war on drugs exists and how civil asset forfeiture contributes to the militarized police state that we have today.

1. Introduction

When discussing whether an agency is doing their job correctly, it is first necessary to define what their job is and which factors determine whether they are doing a good job. There is both private and public (aka government) policing in the United States. The number of private police officers today is greater than the number of public police and is continually growing. For instance, in the 1970s, there were 1.4 public police officers for every private security officer, but this proportion fell to just 0.33 in the 1990s (Zimmerman 2014, 66; Blackstone and Hakim 2013, 157). Taxpayer money is used to pay for public (aka government) police, whereas private police are funded voluntarily, measured in willingness to pay. Since taxpayers are forced to fund public (I use the word 'public' as synonymous with government or state) police, paying for private police means paying twice. Therefore, the increase in private policing represents people's profound dissatisfaction with government police if people are willing to pay twice for protection services. If public police were sufficient, there would be no private police at all, and if the public were satisfied with the government police then the expenditures for private policing ought to decrease, especially since the crime rate is supposedly decreasing (Cook and MacDonald 2010, 5).

According to the National Crime Victimization Survey, which the U.S. Department of Justice uses to measure rates of violent and property crimes and is a survey contacting a large sample of households asking them whether any member of their households, age 12 and over, have become the victims of crimes during the past 6 months and if so to provide details, as Cook and MacDonald show victimization rates for robbery and other violent crimes dropped one-third of its 1994 level by 2004; criminal homicide followed a similar pattern until 1999. Property crime rates declined rapidly since 1980, and according to the NCVS, residential burglaries have declined by 70% since 1976 (Cook and MacDonald 2010, 5). Therefore, the increased demand and supply for private expenditures on private defense is not a result of recent increases in private crime, if the majority of people demanding private defense are aware of or believe that the NCVS report is an accurate measure of crime rates. The demand for private police to deter crime has increased while the supply of criminals has (at least according to the Justice Department) decreased...at least if one measures criminals as engaging in actions that have victims which one can point to. Therefore, it is not unreasonable to conclude that the demand for private defense is more a result of dissatisfaction with public police than a sharp rise in crime where public police resources are simply insufficient.

As I briefly stated in the opening paragraph, before analyzing the role of police, it is important to define what the job of the police is. If the job of the police is to fight crime and protect people from aggression, then how does one measure if the police are successful at doing so? Are an increase in arrest rates a sign of the public police being better at their jobs by being able to catch more thieves or are the arrest rates artificially inflated by increasing the number of victimless crimes and therefore artificially inflating the number of criminals? Or do increasing arrests indicate increasing crime rates, demonstrating a police failure?

Likewise, if the job of the police is to deter crime, then isn't it also possible that an increase in arrests may represent an increase in the number of criminals? Therefore, an increase in arrests shows the police may be more effective at arresting people, but not at deterring crime, for if they were, there ought to be fewer criminals to arrest. According to Lawrence Sherman, *"Instead of watching to prevent crime, motorized police patrol [is] a process of merely waiting to respond to crime."* (Sherman 1983: 149). Also, according to (Zimmerman 2013) and (Blackstone and Hakim 2013), the job of private policing is focused on prevention of crime, whereas the job of public policing is to punish (or arrest) those who commit crimes. Does increasing arrests scare other potential criminals, causing it to decrease crime? Or are the private sectors methods of preventing crime, such as through burglar alarms or selling guns to defend oneself more effective in deterring overall hard crime rates? Since the public police departments obtain their revenue not from willing consumers but from taxation, and civil asset forfeiture, a lack of competition and price mechanism, it is hard to determine whether government police are doing a better job at reducing crime than private defense agencies. Government police agencies don't go out of business or lose money if they fail to satisfy the taxpayer, whereas private defense agencies can be replaced if they fail to satisfy their clients.

The reduction in hard crimes (crimes that have actual victims) since the 1990s has a variety of possible reasons and it is not so clear that the police being better at their job is the primary cause. It is possible that crime rates have been reduced because of better technology produced by the private sector that led to a decrease in crime. It is possible that the crime rate has fallen because of the better angels of our nature or economic growth and a reduction of unemployment in the 1990s. While the causes of a reduction of hard crimes is not so clear and has many possible causes, a simple increase in incarceration and arrest rates by itself does not prove a causal link, especially since the arrest rates for violent and property crimes have decreased, whereas the arrest rates for drug-related (aka victimless) crimes have increased (Benson and Rasmussen 1998: 97). Likewise, the crime rates come from the U.S. Justice Department themselves, and they may have incentives to engage in tactics that cause the crime rate to be artificially deflated. Therefore, the claim that crime rates have fallen may be approached with some skepticism as well since the police agencies are the ones reporting a reduction in hard crimes which they have strong incentives to do since a falling crime rate makes it seem like the police are getting better at their job, therefore encouraging the masses to believe that the police are performing well.

In the following essay, I will talk about the economic incentives of government police, their influence on legislation, their desire to expand the drug war, as well as civil asset forfeiture as an incentive for police to enrich themselves at the expense of people's constitutional rights. Before discussing civil asset forfeiture and the war on drugs, it is first necessary to describe the incentives of police and to look at their behavior and why they act the way they do. Since state police are a bureaucracy and not a competitive market provider, it is necessary to talk about the economic incentives of a bureaucracy in order to explain police behavior. Since state police are not angels, but self-interested people like everyone else, it is necessary to judge the police based on how they act and their incentives which increase the likelihood that they will act that way instead of judging them based on how we would like them to act in an ideal world. Economics is interested in looking at reality, not utopia.

2. Lies, Damn Lies, And Police Statistics or: How I Learned to Stop Worrying and Love Bureaucracy

Police bureaus have a discretionary budget that they get by the bureau's sponsor, such as a legislature overseeing the agency. The bureau's manager can't pursue discretion without constraint *"due to the monitoring and other controls imposed by the bureau's sponsor."* (Benson, Kim, and Rasmussen 1994: 163). There is uncertainty that prevents perfect monitoring, because unlike the market, output is not measurable and can't be objectively evaluated. In order to determine what the discretionary budget should be, the sponsor depends on the bureau to determine which factors are necessary to determine if the goals are being met. For example, the goal of the police bureau is to fight crime. The way to determine if the police are doing a good job fighting crime is by looking at the number of arrests to see how effective the police are. The police are arresting more criminals, so to the public eye, that means more scum off the street and reduced crime. Therefore, in order for the police to have a bigger budget, they have to show the sponsor that they are making more arrests. Police often have quotas on the number of arrests they make that influences their pay. In order for the police to obtain a bigger budget they need to make more arrests and the way to do that is for the police to find more arrestable offenses.

As Koppl and Sacks point out, government police (as all government bureaus do) have a principal–agent problem. The principal–agent problem asks how you make sure that the principal's (the employer or consumer) and agent's (the employee or producer) goals don't conflict. For example, if a principal hires an agent and pays him per hour, how does the principal know the employee is not just taking his time and working slowly to get the job done in order to have more hours to complete the task, and hence more pay? As Kopple and Sacks mention, the solution to the principal-agent problem is that instead of trying to measure inputs, such as hours worked, one measures outputs. If the principle is able to measure not the number of hours worked, but the number of outputs produced and if outputs are easily observable then the way to induce the agent to be more productive is to link one's pay to their output. For example, paying one's tort lawyer a contingency fee ensures that the lawyer has the same desire for a big win as his client does (Koppl and Sacks 2013, 136). Such a way of solving the principal–agent works as long as outcomes are observable.

If, however, some outcomes are observable while others are not, then there is a multitask problem where strong incentives can backfire. In such a case, the agent will have incentives to improve on observable outcomes and neglect unmeasured outcomes. If the unmeasured outcomes matter to the principle, the use of strong incentives (pay based on outcomes) will backfire (Koppl and Sacks 2013, 136). For example, if it's assumed that good grades are a sign of better comprehension of the material, then if a teacher's pay is based on the outcomes of the student's grade, this can cause teachers to indulge in grade inflation or teach easier material in order to artificially get a boost in pay, since the higher grades are easily observable, while improved comprehension of the material is not. Likewise, if arrest rates are used as a proxy for crime rates, then police have incentives to boost arrest rates without making sure that the person they arrest is actually guilty of committing the crime. People who are poor and uneducated have less resources to both understand the laws that exist and be able to pay for a good lawyer. Therefore, police have strong incentives to arrest not necessarily those who are guilty of committing a crime, but those who are less likely to contest the charge or more likely to agree to a plea deal. As Koppl and Sacks state, *"When police investigators have strong incentives to clear cases, they have weaker incentives to discriminate between the guilty and the innocent. Such skewed incentives create the risk of false arrest and conviction. A vital aspect of the proper function of law enforcement is to discriminate between the guilty and the innocent. But the police can clear cases by arresting people who are poor, uneducated, or mentally weak. Such persons may be less able to mount a vigorous defense and more likely to make a false confession"* (Koppl and Sacks 2013, 139).

Police agencies have strong incentives to increase arrest rates. Depending on the political climate, they have incentives to keep crime rates high or low. If there is concern about the police not being effective at their job, there is a strong incentive for the police to show that increasing arrests have led to a reduction in crime rates. However, police agencies also may have incentives to artificially increase the crime rates in order to create a panic to incite demands that the police 'do something' to stop the crime. Of course, the police do not want to eliminate crime entirely or make it seem like there is no need to ramp up police resources to fight crime, because that would cause a decreased perception of the necessity of police, which could lead to a lower budget. If the public, as well as the sponsor overseeing the police agency believe that crime is significantly falling, then the claim that the police budget needs to increase may be met with some skepticism. It's easier to obtain a bigger budget if there is a bigger need. But it's also easier if the sponsor believes that the police are getting better at their jobs and therefore the bigger budget will go to greater use. Therefore, the police have strong incentives to increase arrest rates but not report certain crimes.

For example, in 2009, Adrian Schoolcraft, an NYPD officer, was concerned that the goals of the police department were not consistent with reducing the crime rate, and hence "public safety." In order to prove this, Schoolcraft made audio recordings of all work-related events occurring in his precinct between June 1st 2008-October 31st 2009. Schoolcraft was told to make their quotas of arrests and stop-and-frisks, but not to take certain robbery reports in order to manipulate crime statistics. As one cop says to Schoolcraft, *"A lot of 61s---if it's a robbery, they'll make it a petty larceny. I saw a 61, at T/P/O [time and place of occurrence], a civilian punched in the face, menaced with a gun, and his wallet removed, and they wrote, 'lost property'"* (Koppl and Sacks 2013, 140). As Koppl and Sacks point out, *"The 81st Precinct of Bedford-Stuyvesant had adopted a policy, not sanctioned by the NYPD's official policy, that police officers would not take a complaint from a victim unless the victim would come to the station house in person. If the victim could not come to the station house, then no report was filed and no crime was documented"* (Koppl and Sacks 2013, 140). As such a case reveals, since the crime rates come from the Department of Justice themselves, the reported reduction in hard crimes may not always be based on an accurate reflection of reality as much as political self-interest where police have an incentive to be viewed as being better at their job in order to garner a larger budget. One way to do so is not to report certain crimes or downgrading certain felonies to misdemeanors in order to make it seem like the crime rate is lower than it actually is.

The best way to observe whether the crime rate is falling is to not base the crime rate on reporting from the FBI, but an independent agency. Since an outside observer is not watching the police at all times and observing their behavior, there is no way to know if they are unnecessarily arresting people to boost arrest rates or are refusing to report certain hard crimes in order to make it seem like the crime rate has fallen lower than it actually is. The only way one knows that police are refusing to report certain felonies in Schoolcraft's case is because he had an undercover audio secretly recording police behavior.

While there are cases in which the police officers have incentives to produce statistics showing that the crime rate has fallen in order to show that the police are responsible for a reduction in crime, there are also incentives for police agencies to whip up fear and create new 'crime epidemics' in order to get more resources and funding to combat the crime wave. In 2008, Phoenix police were caught vastly overstating kidnapping statistics, arguing that 358 kidnappings in 2008 were part of a "border crime wave" that threatened to spread across the country if the city did not get more federal money to fight the problem. *"We need federal funding so that we can staff the squads and teams to deal with these violent and deadly crimes,"* Police Chief Jack Harris testified before Congress in 2009 (Shen 2015, 2). Only later did an investigation discover that the actual number of kidnappings in 2008 was closer to 50 than 350. Because of the supposed new crime wave of kidnappings that occurred, the Phoenix police department received $2.4 million in federal grants to deal with border-related crime (Shen 2015, 2).

3. Why a Drug War? The Use of Civil Asset Forfeiture as a Way to Enrich Police Agencies

The incentive of police to create fear and create new crime epidemics is often the case where drug arrests are viewed as preventative measures to reduce crimes since there's a supposed link between drug use and crime. Breton and Wintrobe (1982, 150-151) provide two reasons why bureaucrats advocate policies of directly controlling a source of blame for a problem such as crime (drug prohibition for example) even though such policies have a history of failure and that is: first, there is always opposition to prohibition policies, so when drug prohibition fails to reduce crime, the opponents of the prohibition can be blamed for not doing enough to stop the problem, and secondly, because policy outcomes depend jointly on the inputs of several different groups and bureaus, and the set of possible control methods is very large. When the subset selected fails, the bureau can argue that they selected for a different method to stop the problem which wasn't selected, so the failure is not because of them and that the other groups that were necessary for prohibition to succeed didn't do their share necessary to combat the problem (Benson 1995, 16-17).

According to Boudreaux and Pritchard, interest groups such as politicians and the FBI benefit from outlawing certain commodities. By convincing voters that certain items such as drugs cause crime, such interest groups can get resources including more grant money to get tough on crime in order to decrease drug crimes. According to Boudreaux and Pritchard, there is a cost to prohibiting certain items demanded by consumers: it is politically embarrassing to tax items that the legislators condemn. As they state, *"If the prohibited commodity continues to be distributed, voters may question the politicians' resolve in enforcing the prohibition. In short, legislators feel the pain of foregone tax revenues when they consider prohibiting certain substances, and as a result, generally avoid outright prohibition. Legislators will outlaw only those commodities intensely disliked by large numbers of voters, for only those commodities will yield political benefits outweighing the foregone revenues"* (Boudreaux and Pritchard 1996, 82-83). The use of civil asset forfeiture frees politicians from this political constraint on prohibition since civil asset forfeiture doesn't tax the prohibited commodity but seizes valuable items used as "instrumentalities" in distributing the contraband, many of which are legal (Boudreaux and Pritchard 1996, 82-83). For example, instead of seizing and selling illegal narcotics, the police can, through the use of civil asset forfeiture, declare the money itself guilty of committing a crime, or the car used to pick up and sell the drugs, and then sell the car and transfer such funds to the police department. In other words, instead of taxing illegal substances, which would create negative political backlash, civil asset forfeiture allows police agencies to seize legal items and declare those items guilty of facilitating a crime and then can keep or sell the legal item.

Criminal forfeiture occurs when a person is charged with committing a crime. Criminal forfeiture is known as *'in personam'* (latin for "against a person") crimes which means that the person is considered guilty of committing a crime. Civil forfeitures are *'in rem'* (latin for "against a thing") where an object is considered guilty of committing a crime. Criminal forfeitures require higher standards of proof than civil forfeitures since only humans have rights and objects don't. The Constitution applies to people only, which means that for criminal forfeiture, people are granted constitutional protections before having their assets seized. Criminal forfeiture requires that a person committed the crime is accused and convicted beyond a reasonable doubt, the accused has a right to a trial, it is up to the prosecutor to prove guilt, and only after the accused is proven guilty may his assets that were involved in the criminal act be seized.

Civil forfeiture, on the other hand, doesn't require such high standards before seizing a person's assets. Civil forfeiture only requires probable cause for one's property to be seized (although the protections of civil forfeiture differ from state to state) and the accused has to prove his innocence instead of the prosecutor proving his guilt. Since civil forfeiture requires less evidence and protections than criminal forfeiture, civil asset forfeiture is more vulnerable to abuse than criminal forfeiture.

In order to get tough on drugs and to take the profit out of drug money, the Comprehensive Drug Abuse Prevention and Control Act of 1970 was passed. The funds that the police seized were deposited in the Treasury's General Fund where that money would go to the federal government and be distributed among different government departments to fund various government services (Blumenson and Nilsen 1998, 44). The Comprehensive Crime Control Act of 1984 allowed state and local law enforcement to seize assets that they suspected were used in relation to illegal activity and to have the assets go to the Department of Justice instead of being used in the general fund. Before the Comprehensive Crime Control Act, seized assets were considered property of the government and were to be put in a general fund, but now the proceeds that the police collect can go to the police agencies directly (Chi 2002, 1639).

The goal of the Comprehensive Crime Control Act was to give police incentives to pursue drug crimes by allowing them to keep the seized assets. As Joseph W. Dean of the North Carolina Department of Crime Control and Public Safety bluntly admitted, *"The United States Attorney General...requires that all shared property be used by the transfer for law enforcement purposed. The conflict between state and federal law would prevent the federal government from adopting seizures by state and local agencies...If local and state law enforcement agencies cannot share, the assets will in all likelihood not be seized and forfeited. Thus no one wins but the drug trafficker...If this financial sharing stops, we will kill the goose that laid the golden egg."* (Benson, Rasmussen, and Sollars 1995: 31).

The alleged purpose behind civil asset forfeiture used in the war on drugs is that it would take the profit out of crime by seizing the money and/or items used in commission of a drug deal, thereby taking the profit out of crime. Allowing the police department to keep the property would allow the drug war to be self-financing, thus saving the taxpayers money, since the use of civil asset forfeiture would mean that the drug paraphernalia the police seize could be transferred to the police department and those funds could be used to purchase items that would fund the drug war, instead of having to exclusively rely on taxpayer money to pay for drug enforcement.

Since the police could charge the item, and not the person, guilty of committing a crime, this leads to a lot of abuse since the police don't have to prove the item is guilty, since inanimate objects don't have Constitutional rights, but rather the owner of the item has to prove the item is innocent. Eighty percent of seized items go uncontested, both because the people who own the item have to spend money on lawyers to prove the item is innocent, and because police intimidate people into not contesting the charge. Police tell people that if they just sign a waiver saying that they won't contest the charge, they will be free to go, but if they contest the forfeiture, they will be arrested and charged with a crime. Since many people are both scared and ignorant of the law, they agree to hand over their property to the police and not contest it for fear of being charged with a crime themselves. Such was the case with Delane Johnson in Florida, where he was caught by cops with $10,000 on him. There is an obscure law that says if you have at least $10,000 on you, it must be reported. So, the police accused his money of being drug money but agreed to not accuse him of a drug crime if he signed a waiver not contesting the seizure (Moores 2010: 796). Some would call this armed robbery or extortion, and many would consider it a violation of due process (the presumption of guilt).

Bureaucratic law enforcement interests at the federal, state, and local levels have been important players in the politics of drug control, and a primary source of the information regarding the dangers of certain narcotics. Much of this information is inaccurate and unsubstantiated (Michaels 1987, 311-324), but is used to justify the War on Drugs that exists today thanks to the police bureaucracies (Benson 2008, 38). It is primarily as a result of information propagated by the police that it is now widely believed that drug crime is the root cause of much of what is wrong with society (Benson 2008, 39; Barnett 1984, 53; and the Office of National Drug Control Strategy 1990, 2). The claim that drug use is a primary cause of non-drug crime has been utilized to justify the war on drugs and such a claim has come largely from the police lobbies (Benson 2008, 39). Though as Benson and Rasmussen (1998: 97) show, it is actually drug prohibition that causes the rise in hard crimes, not drug use itself. According to Benson and Rasmussen, as arrest rates for drug arrests increase, it causes a substitution effect for criminals to pursue harder crimes. This is because the odds of them being caught are now lower due to police resources being shifted away from combatting hard crimes and toward pursuing drug seizures and arrests.

People such as Representative Henry Hyde wanted to

reform forfeiture laws by making it harder for police to seize people's assets. Hyde sponsored CAFRA (The Civil Asset Forfeiture Reform Act of 2000). The goal of CAFRA was to require higher standards before being able to seize a person's property. CAFRA shifted the burden of proof from the accused to the prosecutor. Instead of just having probable cause, CAFRA required a preponderance of the evidence needed in order to take away assets, counsel to be provided for the accused, and *"awards attorney's fees to litigants who have substantially prevailed against the government in civil forfeiture proceedings."* (Rulli 2001: 88). While the goal of CAFRA was to offer more protection against the accused, Hyde didn't add provisions to eliminate equitable sharing—which is where state's with higher standards for seizing people's assets than the federal government's standard of preponderance of the evidence can be subject to the federal government's standard if state and federal police work together when it comes to deciding who or what to seize—from the bill due to political lobbying from the police bureaucracy. Law enforcement engaged in a form of rent-seeking by lobbying against any efforts that would reduce the amount of money they could keep from seizures. CAFRA also led to a substantial increase in forfeiture since CAFRA increased the number of offenses that are subject to civil asset forfeiture at the federal level (Kelly and Kole 2013: 6-7).

Because the use of equitable sharing and civil asset forfeiture mainly applies only to drug-related offenses, if police agencies are interested in maximizing their revenue, police resources should go to police seizures and drug arrests relative to other types of crimes, which is exactly what the results show. According to Benson, when the Comprehensive Drug Abuse Prevention and Control Act of 1970 was passed, drug arrests per capita from 1970-1984 were relatively constant. The Comprehensive Crime Control Act of 1984 allowed police to keep a percentage of assets they seize from people they accused of possessing drugs as an incentive for police to make more drug arrests. After the Act, from the years 1984-1989, *"drug arrests per 100,000 population rose by 72 percent."* (Mast, Benson, and

Rasmussen 2000: 287). Therefore, while the war on drugs started in 1970, it wasn't until the 1984 Act which allowed police agencies to benefit from seizing people's belongings they charged with being drug paraphernalia that drug arrests significantly increased.

Hall and Coyne mention that the militarization of domestic policing has its roots in the drug war. In 1981, Congress passed the Military Cooperation with Law Enforcement Act (MCLEA), which both state and local law enforcement overwhelmingly supported. The act calls for the military to assist in helping state and local law enforcement in enforcing drug laws. The MCLEA provided surveillance and support to agencies in the form of aircraft and naval vessels (Hall and Coyne 2013, 495). Therefore, the "drug crisis" provides a clear opportunity for police and military forces to expand their operations, increase their personnel, and expand their discretionary budgets. Police departments grew increasingly dependent on the federal funds granted for anti-drug measures. One program, Community Oriented Policing Services, allocated more than $10 billion to more than 12,000 agencies in less than a decade (Hall and Coyne 2013, 496). A relaxation of drug laws would mean smaller budgets for police and prison-guard unions. As Hall and Coyne point out, in 1980, the number of individuals incarcerated for drug-related offenses was just more than 41,000, whereas today, the number is almost half a million, representing half of all persons in jail or in prison in the U.S.; Such an increase in drug enforcement represents an astonishing 1,100% increase in the number of people incarcerated on drug-related charges (Hall and Coyne 496 2013, 496). Rent-seeking from so-called private prisons (which should more accurately be called rent-seeking crony prisons) and lobbying from the National Fraternal Order of Police convinced Congress in 2008 to increase the penalties for particular types of narcotics (Hall and Coyne 496 2013, 496).

The availability of military technologies for domestic use with the National Defense Authorization Act of Fiscal Year 1997 with the creation of the 1033 Program allows, *"all law enforcement agencies to acquire property for bona fide law enforcement purposed that assist in their arrest and apprehension mission [and that] preference is given to counter-drug and counter-terrorism requests"* (Boettke, Palagashvili, and Piano 2017, 926). The 1033 Program incentivizes police agencies to continue to pursue the drug war since the police agencies would only get such "free" and "cheap" items such as pistols, rifles, ammunition, aviation parts, night-vision goggles, personnel carriers, boats, aircraft parts, and body armor, if the state and local police departments engaged in counter-drug measures. According to the guidelines of the 1033 Program, participating police departments are required to use any transferred equipment within one year of receiving them, otherwise they must return the military equipment to the feds. Since such equipment could only be used for drug busts, such a program further encourages police agencies to engage in SWAT raids and drug busts in order for them to keep such military equipment (Boettke, Palagashvili, and Piano 2017, 929). The first SWAT team was used in 1969, but the practice became common in the 1980s. During the 1970s, there were about 300 SWAT raids per year. In 2005, there were about 100 to 150 per day. There was a fifty percent increase in the number of paramilitary units (PPUs) in SWAT raids and a fivefold increase in the deployment of those units between 1980 and 1995; and as of 2000, more than 80% of the deployment of PPUs were justified by the war on drugs (Boettke, Palagashvili, and Piano 2017, 928). The use of civil asset forfeiture to combat drug "crimes" began in 1984, although the enforcement of the war on drugs and the use of SWAT raids and PPUs began in 1970. It's no coincidence that the use of civil asset forfeiture lead to an enormous increase in uninvited and unannounced SWAT raids on people's property as well as leading to military style of policing, since such monetary incentives encourage the police to engage in no-knock raids, especially when they are able to petition to Congress and influence legislation that weakens people's civil liberties as a necessary means to combat the drug war. As Benson points out, the 1984 federal civil asset forfeiture law was a bureaucratically-demanded legislative act which was pursued as a means to expand police powers. Among the supporters of the 1984 Act allowing police agencies to transfer seized assets to the police department were the U.S. Customs Service, various police departments and sheriffs, and the U.S. Drug Enforcement Administration; while there was no representation of local government oversight authorities opposing such legislation (Benson 2008, 41).

As a result of stiffer penalties for drug offenses, people in prison for hard crimes are being let out earlier than their sentences called for in order to make room for those being criminalized for drug "crimes." An example of such a case is Frank Potts, who was released from the Florida prison system in 1988, after serving six years of a fifteen-year sentence for molesting an eleven-year-old girl, despite the report of a parole examiner who noted there was a very high probability of recidivism if Potts was released. After Potts was released early in order to make room for a person arrested of a drug crime, there was an intense investigation that Potts had not only molested another eleven year old girl after being released early, but he had allegedly also killed as many as thirteen people (Benson and Rasmussen 1996, 185).

Increased drug enforcement causes an increase in crime. This is because prohibition creates cartels and artificially inflates the prices of drugs, thereby making it more beneficial for people to supply the drugs since there is a greater profit. Additionally, prohibition may reduce competition by running the narcotic market underground as a black market. Another way drug prohibition increases crime is by reducing the costs of pursuing hard crimes, because every cop enforcing a drug law represents a cop not stopping hard crimes, such as robbery, murder, and rape. Having police resources being used to increase drug arrests reduces the costs of entering into hard crime since such criminals are now less likely to get caught, so assuming criminals themselves are rational, going after victimless crimes increases crimes with actual victims since fewer resources are available to combat it. Likewise, the claim that drug use increases crime is murky indeed. While it may very well be true that many violent criminals also engage in drug use, this does not prove that it is the drug use that is causing them to pursue a life of crime. According to the Bureau of Justice statistics, surveys of prison inmates found that approximately half of the inmates who had ever used a major drug and three-fifths of those who used a major drug regularly did not do so until after their first arrest for some non-drug crime (Benson 2008, 6)—that is "after their criminal career had begun" (Innes 1988, 1-2). Another large scale survey of jail inmates found that more than half who reported regular drug use said that their first arrest for a crime occurred an average of two years before their first use of drugs (Benson 2008, 6; Harlow 1991, 7). Therefore, while it may be the case that many criminals use drugs, most of them seem to use the drugs after they have turned to crime and not before. If such is the case, then drugs can't cause crime if the crime is committed before the drug use.

4. Private and Public Police Differences

As shown above in quite some detail, police agencies are a bureaucracy and the goal of the bureaucracy is to expand their budget and size. Any decrease in spending results in a lower budget the following year. Therefore, there is little incentive to engage in behavior that will reduce their costs. Since the sponsor has a multitask problem where he can't oversee the actions of those in the agency, and since those in the agency have some outcomes which are observable and others which are not, once arrest rates become a proxy for measuring crime, police agencies have incentives to make a lot of arrests to expand their budgets. Such distorted incentives cause police agencies to lobby and influence in support of legislation that increases the number of arrestable offenses so that more resources can be dedicated to combat the new crime epidemic. Such bureaucratic self-interest explains why it is totally rational for police lobbies to play a big role in expanding the drug war. The more crimes that exist, the more resources are given to them to fight against such crimes. Since the government police obtain their revenue irrespective of job performance and since police unions have successfully lobbied to have government police get paid at least as much as private police agencies (Blackstone and Hakim 2013) and (Benson 1995) their pay is not based on willingness to pay by market consumers but based on political incentives. The next question to ask and try to answer is the difference between how private defense acts to deter crime versus government police actions to deter crime.

As stated earlier, police agencies are in the business of having arrest quotas and punishing people for committing crimes, whereas private defense is in the business of deterring crimes. Though expenditures on private defense are increasing and are greater than expenditures on public defense, the wages of private security are 47% lower than what public officers earn (Blackstone and Hakim 2013, 160). When private security guards replaced public security guards escorting prisoners, it led to a cost savings of 50% (Blackstone and Hakim 2013, 160). Since private security is subject to competition and profit and loss, they have an incentive to cut costs while maintaining quality. Since private defense agencies have competitors, in order to stay in business, they have to be better than their competitors. As Zimmerman points out, shopping centers may employ private security primarily to prevent shoplifting and theft, but also to offer a safer environment than their competitors in order to attract customers. Since customers value a secure and safe environment, businesses that have a reputation for being safer than their competitors can not only get more business, but reflect the gains of a safer environment in the cost of the products they sell, such as higher ticket prices at a movie theater (Zimmerman 2014, 67). If competing businesses improve their security but others fail to and as a result a crime occurs due to having insufficient private defense, the business in question risks loss of clientele by not improving its own security (Blackstone and Hakim 2013, 162). Such a loss of revenue reveals the market costs that come from not having competent security, whereas the mayor of a city doesn't lose his job or get a demotion if the crime level should rise in his town because the government police fail to adequately defend the citizenry. In fact, typically, an increase in crime in a "public" area leads to bigger budgets for the city in order to better combat them next time, as 71 task forces were added after the terrorist attacks on 9/11 (Hall and Coyne 2013, 497). Also, unlike many government police agencies which wear uniforms, private security officers could wear plainclothes, making it harder for potential criminals to detect who is a security officer and who is not. *"Uncertainty about where such security efforts are deployed could lead to a general deterrence effect"* (Zimmerman 2014, 67).

Since government police receive guaranteed revenue from taxation, they have no incentive to cut costs or even measure whether they are benefitting the taxpayers, because the taxpayers don't control the police. For example, even though drug enforcement is increasing, public perception on drug arrests being an effective way to deal with drug use is in conflict. In a 1990 Gallup Poll, only 4% of people thought that more money combating drugs should be spent on arresting users and only 19% supported arresting sellers, whereas 40% thought using the funds to educate people against drugs was more effective in combating drug use. Likewise, 57% of those asked in 1989 thought building more federal prisons would not reduce illegal drug use, while 80% thought more money for drug treatment would be effective (Benson and Rasmussen 1996, 184). Yet despite what public opinion may say, the drug war persists. Therefore, unlike private defense, public police are not subject to the wishes of the taxpayers (not to mention that the taxpayers are individuals and not an aggregate unit).

Private defense has an incentive to benefit their client and invest and engage in technology that reduces their clients' risk of property damage. For example, LoJack is a private security device that can be placed on a person's vehicle in order to deter theft. LoJack claims a 90% recovery rate for one's stolen car, compared with a 63% chance of recovery of a typical car without LoJack (Cook and MacDonald 2010,

12-13). Ayres and Levitt (1998) found that each dollar spent on LoJack resulted in a reduction in the costs of auto theft of about $10.

Helland and Tabarrok (2004) compared private bail bondsmen to public law enforcement and found that bail bondsmen were more effective in reducing the failure to appear rates for a trial than public bail officers. Bail bondmen were also more successful at capturing those who were charged with a felony but failed to appear in court than government police. According to Helland and Tabarrock, *"Bond dealers...recognize that what make their pursuit of skips most effective is the time they devote to the task. In contrast, public police are often strained for resources, and the rearrests of defendants who fail to show up at trial is usually given low precedence"* (Helland and Tabarrok 2004, 98).

In Conclusion

The main problem with government police (and there are many) is not only how does one know whether the police are doing a better job than the alternative since there is no price mechanism, competition, and profit and loss on which to determine if they are doing a better job than their competitors, but another problem with government police is the the types of "crimes" or legislation that police decide to go after. Private police have a client and their client is interested in protecting his property. The crimes that such private defense agents are likely to pursue are those which have victims. A person is unlikely to spend money to hire someone to stop his neighbor from engaging in harmless actions that he finds objectionable, but instead will spend resources to protect himself and his property. Since the government police have an incentive to perpetually grow their budgets, the way to do so is not by showing that crime is being reduced through their actions, since such monitoring is not possible and can't be objectively evaluated. The government police are viewed as being effective at their job based on their arrest rates and clearing cases, which means they have an incentive not to defend people, but to arrest people. The more arrests they make, the more they are viewed by the sponsor as being good at their job, which means they have an incentive to make lots of arrests, but not necessarily to prevent crimes. Likewise, government police have incentives to increase the number of arrestable offenses in order to get a larger discretionary budget. As mentioned above, the police lobbies, unions, and bureaus were big supporters of making narcotics illegal as well as finding out and presenting information that such narcotics were harmful, while ignoring studies that revealed the opposite.

The problem with making voluntary transactions into crimes is, in the words of Naylor, *"Police action [is being] shifted from combating predatory offenses practiced against an unwilling public to attacking enterprise crimes in which underground economies attempted to service the [now] forbidden consumption needs for a complicit public."* (Naylor 2000: 8). Even more importantly, *"Though both are lumped together as co-equals in the criminal code, enterprise crimes [aka victimless crimes, such as drugs] have an economic nature and social impact that is radically different from predatory ones. Enterprise crimes involve the production and/or distribution of new goods and services that happen to be illegal by their very nature...Since the transfers are voluntary, it is often difficult to define a "victim," unless it is some abstract (and largely meaningless) construct like "society." Although the total sums involved are often* **claimed** *to be considerable, in absolute terms and in relation to the economy as a whole, as long as the transactions remain voluntary, there are no monetary loses to any individual from the act itself (although there may be from indirect consequences from the act). On the contrary, because enterprise crimes involve production and distribution of new goods and services...they raise national income and...contribute to economic welfare. Their morality is accordingly debatable."* (Naylor 2000: 9).

In other words, how does one measure the damage caused by drug-related offenses? In a society where only crimes which had tangible victims were illegal, there would be a way to measure the damage done by such actions in a few possible ways: one is by seeing the damage the actions caused and measuring it, and likewise in such cases, the victim would call the cops and report a crime, whereas with the war on drugs and other victimless crimes, police units are called by their supervisors to stop a drug bust. Instead of only responding to calls by a victim, with the war on drugs, police can be sent out in order to make arrests by their supervisor. But in such a case, how does one measure the damage caused by drug crimes if there is no victim pursuing it? Likewise, no person can be at two places at once, and resources are limited, so if a police officer gets a call from a victim to stop a domestic violence incident or a call from their supervisor to go to make a drug bust, who decides which action ought to take precedence? Should the police respond to victims first and their supervisors next (if at all)? And since police can be demoted or promoted by their supervisors but not by civilians calling them complaining about a violent incident or a thief, what incentive is there for the government police to be most responsive to those who call him over his supervisors?

Drug prohibition influences the actions of others. Drug prohibition not only leads to hard crimes, but the creation of synthetic drugs which are not currently illegal, but may very well be more harmful than the drugs which are currently illegal. Such synthetic drugs may only exist because the original formulations have been made illegal and hence the supply is artificially constrained, forcing people to create substitutes. Drug arrests lower the costs of other types of crimes, especially when drug arrests are increasing more than hard crimes. When government police go after drug dealers and sellers, it causes a substitution effect in which hard crimes become more preferable to commit since the odds of being captured are lower. When a product that people value becomes illegal, this creates costs on those who want to buy and sell the drug, as well as increasing the odds of police bribery and corruption (Sisk 1982). Every person in prison for a victimless crime is a person not in the market creating value and who knows what they may have invented or discovered if not kept in a government cage. Such costs must be taken into account when measuring the costs of the drug war, but when the supply is created by the bureau themselves and not a consumer, then how can such a cost-benefit analysis be accurately measured? Any output not willingly demanded, measured in willingness to pay makes it where the benefits of government police are impossible to measure since their services are not paid for by willing customers and if you are dissatisfied with the services the government police are providing you, you are unable to cancel your subscription to the FBI.

References

1) Ayres, Ian, and Steven D. Levitt. "Measuring positive externalities from unobservable victim precaution: an empirical analysis of Lojack." *The Quarterly Journal of Economics* 113.1 (1998): 43-77.

2) Barnett, Randy E. "Review essay/public decisions and private rights." *Criminal Justice Ethics* 3.2 (1984): 50-62.

3) Benson, Bruce L. "Understanding bureaucratic behavior: Implications from the public choice literature." *Journal of Public Finance and Public Choice* 8.2-3 (1995): 89-117.

4) Benson, Bruce L., and DeVoe Moore. "The war on drugs: a public bad." *Searle Center on Law, Regulation, and Economic Growth, Northwestern University Law School, Chicago, IL* (2008).

5) Benson, Bruce L., Illjoong Kim, and David W. Rasmussen. "Estimating Deterrence Effects: A Public Choice Perspective on the Economies of Crime." *Southern Economic Journal*, Vol. 61, No. 1, Southern Economic Association, (July 1994), pp. 161-168.

6) Benson, Bruce L. and David W. Rasmussen. "Deterrence and Public Policy: Trade-Offs in the Allocation of Police Resources." *International Review of Law and Economics*, New York: Elsevier Science Inc., 1998, pp. 77-100.

7) Benson, Bruce L., and David W. Rasmussen. "Predatory public finance and the origins of the war on drugs: 1984–1989." *The Independent Review* 1.2 (1996): 163-189.

8) Benson, Bruce L., David W. Rasmussen, and David L. Sollars. "Police Bureaucracies, Their Incentives, and the War on Drugs." *Public Choice*, Vol. 83. No. 1/2.. Kluwer Academic Publishers: Netherlands, (April 1995), pp. 21-45.

9) Blackstone, Erwin A., and Simon Hakim. "Competition versus monopoly in the provision of police." *Security journal* 26.2 (2013): 157-179.

10) Blumenson, Eric and Eva Nilsen. "Policing for Profit: The Drug War's Hidden Economic Agenda." *The University of Chicago Law Review*, Vol. 65, No., 1998, pp. 35-114.

11) Boettke, Peter J., Liya Palagashvili, and Ennio E. Piano. "Federalism and the Police: An Applied Theory of Fiscal Attention." *Ariz. St. LJ* 49 (2017): 907.

12) Boudreaux, Donald J., and Adam C. Pritchard. "Civil forfeiture and the war on drugs: Lessons from economics and history." *San Diego L. Rev.* 33 (1996): 79.

13) Chi, Karis Ann-Yu. "Follow the Money: Getting to the Root of the Problem with Civil Asset Forfeiture in California." *California Law Review*, Vol. 90, No. 5 (Oct., 2002), pp. 1635-1673.

14) Cook, Philip J., and John MacDonald. *Public safety through private action: an economic assessment of bids, locks, and citizen cooperation.* No. w15877. National Bureau of Economic Research, 2010.

15) Hall, Abigail R., and Christopher J. Coyne. "The militarization of US domestic policing." *The Independent Review* 17.4 (2013): 485-504.

16) Harlow, C. W., et al. "Drugs and jail inmates, 1989." (1991).

17) Helland, Eric, and Alexander Tabarrok. "The fugitive: Evidence on public versus private law enforcement from bail jumping." *The Journal of Law and Economics* 47.1 (2004): 93-122.

18) Innes, Christopher A. "Drug use and crime." *Washington, DC, US Department of Justice* (1988).

19) Kelly, Brian D. and Maureen A. Kole. "The Effects of Asset Forfeiture on Policing: A Panel Approach." (December 2013), pp. 1-35.

20) Koppl, Roger, and Meghan Sacks. "The criminal justice system creates incentives for false convictions." *Criminal Justice Ethics* 32.2 (2013): 126-162.

21) Mast, Brent D., Bruce L. Benson, and David W. Rasmussen. "Entrepreneurial Police and Drug

Enforcement Policy." *Public Choice*, Netherlands: Kluwer Academic Publishers, 2000, pp. 285-308.

22) Moores, Eric. "Reforming the Civil Asset Forfeiture Reform Act." *Arizona Law Review*, Vol. 51, 2009, pp. 777-803.

23) Naylor, R. Tom. "Wash-out: A critique of follow-the-money methods in crime control policy." *Crime, Law and Social Change* 32.1 (1999): 1-58.

24) Rulli, Louis S. "The Long Term Impact of CAFRA: Expanding Access to Counsel and Encouraging Greater Use of Criminal Forfeiture." *Federal Sentencing Reporter*, Vol. 14, No. 2, Forfeiture: Recent Reform and Future Outlook, University of California Press: Vera Institute of Justice, (September/October 2001), pp. 87-97.

25) Shen, Aviva. "What Happens When People Panic About Crime Rates" *Think Progress*, 2015. https://thinkprogress.org/what-happens-when-p eople-panic-about-crime-rates-8ef19aae2a0b/

26) Sherman, Lawrence W. "Patrol strategies for police." *Crime and public policy* 145 (1983).

27) Sisk, David E. "Police corruption and criminal monopoly: Victimless crimes." *The Journal of Legal Studies* 11.2 (1982): 395-403.

28) Wintrobe, A. Breton-R. "The logic of bureaucratic conduct." *An Analysis* (1982).

29) Zimmerman, Paul R. "The deterrence of crime through private security efforts: theory and evidence." *International Review of Law and Economics* 37 (2014): 66-75.

Daniel Rothschild

Anarchy: The Lesser of Two Evils

Abstract: Is the existence of the nation-state responsible for freer societies and a decrease in violence? Looking at Somalia pre-anarchy and Somalia post-anarchy allows one to compare and contrast to see if things improved in the state's absence. Failures of exporting democracy and imposing law from above reveals how culture and social norms are a greater influence on people's behavior and the type of society one lives under than government legislation. The law in the West, often considered a paragon of justice and freedom, was not a creation of the state, but arose spontaneously. Commercial, merchant, and the common law arose privately. The rule of law is not a state creation, but a result of spontaneous order that arose in order for people to engage in reciprocity and coexist harmoniously with each other.

I. Introduction

For many, law and government are synonyms and can't exist independently of each other. To argue against the existence of government is often presumed to argue against the existence of law. Lon Fuller defines law as, *"a direction of purposive human effort, consists in the enterprise of subjecting human conduct to the governance of rules"* (Fuller 1964, 30). Based on such a definition, law and government are separate concepts. Laws are the rules of the game, and government is an institution that can enforce them. Just like food and supermarkets are not synonyms, neither are laws and governments. I define a government similarly to how Max Weber defined it. A government or state is an institution that holds a legitimized monopolization of force within a given territorial area. Anarchy is the absence of a state. To clarify, government is the monopolization of law, and anarchy is the polycentric development of law. A society without a state is not necessarily a society without laws, but a society without a monopoly rulemaking enforcer.

There are many reasons to oppose the government and instead prefer a polycentric legal system. One is that competition is preferable to uniformity. Another reason is that since the government gets guaranteed revenue by a compulsory levy known as taxation, as well as being able to forcibly prevent competition, the government is not bound by satisfying the needs of the people. If a person does not have to compete and gets a guaranteed income, there is less of an incentive to do well than if one had to persuade people to buy their services. The reason that the market is superior to the state is because the market has competition, which requires firms to persuade people to hand over their money, whereas the government can forcibly expropriate it. If the government can force people to hand over their money irrespective of job performance, the government has less of an incentive to provide a good product or service then it would if getting money from people was not a guarantee, but based on providing a more valuable service than the money one chooses to fork over. The type of social organization I am advocating for is referred to as anarcho-capitalism, where courts, police, and money are determined by market forces, not politics. I want to privatize everything. Just like schools, food, healthcare, and automobiles increase in quality when they are supplied by the market, so too does protection services. I advocate a polycentric legal system, where the market determines law, not legislative bodies.

The purpose of this paper is to present my case for why a stateless society is superior to one ruled by a government. Before going over the empirical evidence to show how law originally existed in the absence of a state and in certain areas still does, it is first necessary to go over the methodology on how to answer: Is the existence of the nation-state responsible for a free society?

In order to answer the question of whether the state is both superior and necessary to a society without one, it is first necessary to address the issue of how freedom is maximized. Daniel Klein rejects the axiom view of liberty which says that direct liberty should never be violated. Instead, he takes the maxim view of liberty, which is that by and large direct liberty should never be violated. Usually there is not a tension between direct liberty and overall liberty, but there may be cases where they are in conflict. When there is tension between direct and overall liberty, Daniel Klein says that the liberty principle should advocate for whichever is more liberty augmenting. According to Daniel Klein, *"The liberty principle says: In a choice between a pair of policy reforms (one of which may be no reform at all), the reform that ranks higher in liberty is more desirable"* (Klein 2012, 245). Daniel Klein says that what constitutes such an outlook is the liberty maxim, which is that by and large the liberty principle holds. Instead of taking a 100% rule of coercion that is never justified, Daniel Klein advocates for a presumption of liberty. According to Klein, *"that presumption places the burden of proof on those who would favor the less-liberty choice"* (Klein 2012, 246). Klein stresses that just because a principle does not work 100% of the time does not mean it should be rejected for a principle that vainly tries to be applicable in all cases. By and large is sufficient.

Daniel Klein's presumption of liberty is a good rule of thumb. Don't commit coercion unless there is a common sense reason for doing so. If there is a way to solve an issue without a violation of direct liberty, the peaceful alternative should be chosen instead. I accept Daniel Klein's view of liberty. The disagreement lies in that the maxim view of liberty is somehow a justification for the government's existence. Daniel Klein supports a nightwatchman state, yet the presumption of liberty does not only not require a limited government, but ought to presume anarchy. Daniel Klein mentions Randy Barnett and David Friedman as people who share his presumption of liberty view. Both Barnett and Friedman are anarchists.

Anarchist philosopher Michael Huemer agrees with Klein's presumption of liberty and believes that coercion may be justified in certain cases. An example Huemer gives is a lifeboat situation where the only way to get people to remove water from the lifeboat is by pointing a gun at them (he also mentions stealing a car in order to drive a critical patient to the hospital). Huemer says, "*Your entitlement to coerce is highly specific and content-dependent: it depends upon your having a correct (or at least well-justified) plan for saving the boat, and you may coerce others only to induce cooperation with that plan. More precisely, you must at least be justified in believing that the expected benefits of coercively imposing your plan on others are very large and much larger than the expected harms. You may not coerce others to induce harmful or useless behaviors or behaviors designed to serve ulterior purposes unrelated to the emergency. For instance, if you display your firearm and order everyone to start scooping water into the boat, you are acting wrongly – and similarly if you use the weapon to force the others to pray to Poseidon, lash themselves with belt, or hand over $50 to your friend Sally...If, therefore, we rely upon cases like this to account for the state's right to coerce or violate the property rights of its citizens, the proper conclusion is that the state's legitimate powers must be highly specific and content-dependent*" (Huemer 2013,

94-95). Huemer also mentions that such a scenario fails to justify political authority since a government as stated above is a monopolization of the use of force. If there are certain situations where *"sometimes coercion is our friend"* (Klein & Clark 2012, 134), then why does it matter who does the coercion? If there are certain situations where coercion is justified in order to increase overall liberty, it is based on the situation, not on who does it. Klein (at least in his paper on overall vs. direct liberty) has not justified the night watchman state. Klein has done an excellent job arguing for why coercion may be justified in certain cases, but not why it is licit for the state to use force in areas where it would be illicit for others to do so. If there are certain situations where it may be justified to steal bread, why is it justified for government to steal the bread, but not for a private individual? In other words, what is the reason it is okay for A to coerce B, but not for anyone else to coerce B? The situation ought to determine when coercion is justified, not who is doing the coercing. If there are certain situations where coercion is justified, it is justified for anyone, not just the government. Therefore, the presumption of liberty, far from justifying the existence of monopoly enforcement over polycentric law, has only justified certain cases where coercion is justified. Perhaps the reply will be that the reason the government should be able to use force where it would be illegal for anyone else to do so is that the liberty principle would increase if only government is given this unique power. It is this question that my paper will explore. Now onto the methodology.

II. Methodology

One of the most comprehensive studies examining why violence has decreased was conducted by Steven Pinker in his mammoth tome, *The Better Angels of Our Nature*. Steven Pinker does not attribute the decline of violence solely to the existence of the nation-state. Rather, the nation-state is one reason among others that accounts for the decline of homicide per capita. An increase in commerce and an increase in the use of reason are also contributing factors. Pinker discusses the *"the Flynn effect,"* which is where people today are given the same IQ test as in generations past. James Flynn studied IQ scores throughout different regions of the world and the results were the same everywhere: IQ has increased throughout the 20th century globally. According to Pinker, "*An average teenager today, if he or she could time-travel back to 1910, would have had an IQ of 130, and [a] typical person of 1910, if time-transported forward to the present, would have a mean IQ of 70*" (Pinker 2011, 310). According to Aschwin de Wolf, one possible biological explanation for why violence has declined, which Pinker neglects to mention, is that biological evolution takes those who are more prone to violence out of the gene pool. As commerce increases and society adopts conventions that reward cooperation over force, those most prone to violence have fewer reproductive advantages and are disproportionately removed from the gene pool. Even in the case of a military draft, biological evolution may be a factor for those more prone to violence being removed from the gene pool since conscription selects men who value honor and are more likely to engage in risky behavior (Wolf 2012, 131).

One major problem with looking at the decline of violence throughout history and showing that current societies with a nation-state have a lower homicide rate per capita than primitive nongovernmental societies centuries ago is that such data confuses causation for correlation. Is the decline in violence caused by the existence of the nation-state or is violence declining for other reasons and would have declined even more if not for the nation-state? To use an example: Suppose someone argues for government regulation and uses the existence of government regulation over automobiles to justify regulation over other industries. The person argues as follows: Cars today have more regulation than the first Model-T Ford car. Regulation over the automobile industry has increased and so has car safety. The cars today are safer and of better quality than the earlier unregulated cars, therefore, automobile regulation increases car safety and quality.

One possible flaw is that the argument ignores the fact that there is a tendency for products to improve over time. One possible reason that automobiles today are safer and better than the first automobiles is because the automobile manufacturers of today are able to stand on the shoulders of giants. They are able to see what previous automobile makers have created, examine any errors, and correct them. Today's generation of car makers learned from previous generations and improved on them, using information today that was not available in the past. There are many possibilities for why cars are safer today other than government regulation. Is government regulation the cause of the increase in car safety and quality? Or has car safety and quality increased along with increased government regulation and would have increased as much or even more in its absence? In other words, are today's cars better because of government regulation or in spite of government regulation? Similarly is the decline of violence because of the existence of the nation-state or in spite of the existence of the nation-state? Simply saying there is less violence now than in the past is not sufficient to answer such a question.

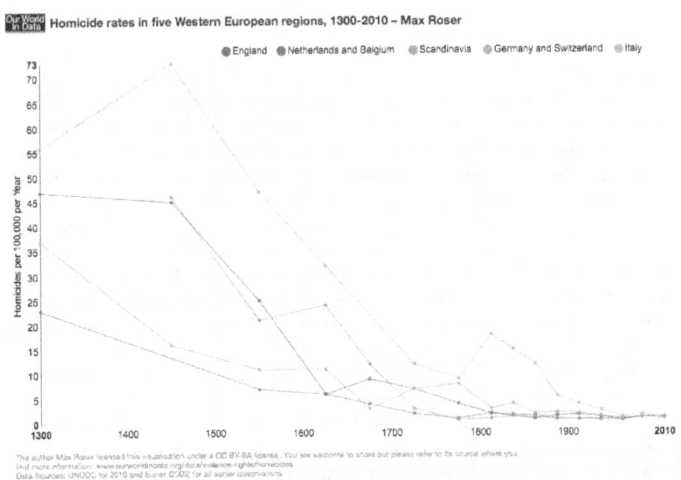

As the above graph shows, out of the five countries, England has the lowest homicide rate. There has been a major decline in violence in England since the mid-1500s. What is interesting about the above graph is that from the 1500s until the mid-1800s, policing has been mostly a responsibility of private individuals. It wasn't until 1737 when taxes were used to pay for public police when King George II used taxpayer money to hire watchmen (Benson 1990, 74). However government control of policemen was not introduced in London until 1829, when Robert Peel introduced the Metropolitan Police Act. The legislation established the first modern police force in England (Benson 1990, 74). Yet, parts of London still had a private police force. The nationalization, nationwide police force in London was created in 1856 (Koyama 2012, 15). Even though public policing did not begin until 1856, as Max Roser's graph above shows, the crime in England fell long before the arrival of public police. Therefore, it is not sufficient to determine that homicide rates decreased as a result of the nation-state.

Another flawed methodology compares any current day anarchist society with a current day society with a nation-state. If one for example, compares present day "anarchist" Somalia with current day United States and concludes that the United States is superior, this does not show the superiority of a nation-state. One must compare apples to apples. Just like it would be disingenuous to use North Korea as an example of government failing, so too would it be disingenuous to use current day Somalia as an example in order to prove the superiority of government. Not all societies are the same. There is no reason to presume that all anarchist societies would be similar any more than there is to conclude that all societies with a nation-state would be similar.

The annual *Fragile States Index*[15] ranks 178 countries based on social, economic, and political indicators to see how capable states are in terms of solving their own problems

---

[15] http://fsi.fundforpeace.org/rankings-2015

and how many states are on the verge of collapse. Of the 178 states ranked in 2015, 38 have an "alert" status, 87 are in "warning" mode, 12 are "less stable," 26 are "stable," and only 15 states are considered "sustainable" (with Finland being the only state which is considered "very sustainable"). Therefore, if one takes the nonpartisan *Fragile States Index* as a guide, the majority of nation-states are failing to provide peace, stability, protection, and liberty to their citizenry. An effective, protective, liberty augmenting government is the exception, not the rule.

Daniel Hannan credits the nation-state for the existence of freedom. He states that *"It is extremely rare to find justice, freedom, or representative government flourishing in any context other than a nation-state"* (Hannan 2013, 66). Yet, even Hannan admits that the majority of nation-states are not successful and that freedom primarily resides among the 11% residing in the Anglosphere and the closely related and largely Protestant states of Nordic and Germanic origin. (Hannan 2013, 313-314). Thus, while Hannan may credit the existence of liberty and justice to the creation of nation-states, it is only a certain kind of nation-state. The vast majority of nation-states do not in fact protect liberty and justice, so the success of these countries must be due to something other than simply the creation of the nation-state.

A better methodology than simply comparing any current nation-state with any current anarchist society or comparing primitive societies with modern day societies is instead to compare apples to apples. Instead of comparing a modern industrialized country to a third-world country, it would be better to compare the same country within around the same time span. For example, instead of comparing present-day New Zealand to present-day Somalia, it would be better to compare Somalia from when they had a government—from the years 1969-1991—and when Somalia was without a government—from the years 1991-2005. Such a comparison allows one to compare the same area with roughly the same people, with roughly the same time period. Comparing the same area from one decade or two to the next, one gets a clearer comparison than they would when comparing over a much wider net. Comparing the same region, with roughly the same people, same history, and same background allows one to see how the same region fares under anarchy compared to the existence of a government.

My claim is a rather modest and weak one. I am not claiming that any area without a nation-state is superior to any area with one. I am claiming that the existence of a government does not necessarily improve society and that by removing the government, people will generally be better off. For example, I am not claiming that people in anarchist Somalia or <u>anarchist Zomia</u>[16] are better off than the people in New Zealand or the United States, but rather the people in Somalia without a state are better off than those Somalians with one. Such a comparison focuses on the existence of government within an area and seeing if its removal made people better off or worse off. As I will show later, liberty is augmented when people under a government (like the Somalians) have their government removed, people are better off under a smaller government than a bigger one, and the places where government is newest are better off than in countries where the government has been around longer. In other words, liberty is augmented when the government is either nonexistent, smaller, or has been in existence for a shorter duration. If government is a positive force that augments overall liberty, then why would the same people's living standards increase when government decreases? If the existence of the state is necessary in order to have liberty and freedom, then why are the states that emerged first and are older more backwards than the more recent states?

III. The Creation of The Common Law, Commercial Law and Societies without a Government

---

[16]

medium.com/@matthijsbijl/welcome-to-zomia-the-anarchist-co untry-youve-never-heard-of-6d2172da8ef3

It is not the existence of government (or to use a modern euphemism, "the law") that is responsible for relatively free societies, but cultural norms and institutions are the main driving forces that determine the relative freedom people enjoy. It is not the imposition of government creation and enforcement of laws that generate freedom, but cultural norms where the majority of people respect property and individual rights. It is not the government that creates cultural and societal norms, but rather the laws that people respect and follow are a reflection of the societal norms that are already in existence. There are areas with polycentric legal systems that protect people and property with relatively little violence and there have been anarchist societies with a lot of violence and property rights that failed to be protected. Likewise, there are nation-states where property rights are relatively protected and nation-states where the very concept of individual rights is non-existent. The rule of law (aka a monopolistic legal system) is not responsible for a reduction in violence, but cultural norms where individual rights take precedence over the fictional rights of society. Individual rights can be prevalent in both anarchist and non-anarchist societies, but since government is more powerful than decentralization, the violation of individual rights is likely to be more severe under a nation-state than within an anarchist society.

To determine whether social norms are exogenous to the government, one needs to see if societal norms and institutions exist in the absence of a state. If so, this would imply that the state is not a necessary condition for the emergence of cultural and societal norms. Three examples where legal order arose prior to the existence of nation-states are medieval Iceland, the California Gold Rush, and medieval merchant society. The existence of these three cases shows that *"it is problematic to identify law with centralized coercion"* (Hadfield & Weingast 2012, 3).

From the 10th to 13th centuries, Iceland's legal system was totally privatized, and developed without any central authority. The laws were made by a "parliament," in which the seats of the legislature were held by the owners of the boroughs, or by men chosen by them (Friedman 1979, 401). Such 'chieftains' were known as goooros, and they presided over groups of men that agreed to follow them and be members of that congregation. Every man was part of a congregation and could name his chief, and could change congregations at any time. This ability to become elected to the legislature by leading a congregation became *"a marketable property"* that could be *"given away, sold, held by a partnership, inherited, or whatever* (Friedman 1979, 405).

During this time, many of the inhabitants of Iceland came from Norway after deciding to leave King Harald Fairhair's rule. The laws and "political" system that developed were based on Norwegian traditions and the Anglo-Saxon common law. There were no crimes against 'society', only crimes against individuals. There was no executive body and no prosecuting attorney by the state. Prosecution was the responsibility of the individuals harmed or their heirs. When a conflict arose, there were private courts where half of the members of the court were chosen by the plaintiff and half by the defendant (Friedman 1979, 404). If the court ruled against the defendant, it was his responsibility to pay the assigned punishment, which was almost always a fine. If he did not pay the fine, he was considered an outlaw. People declared to be an outlaw were unable to be sheltered, and those who did shelter an outlaw could be prosecuted for doing so.

A possible objection to private law enforcement is that it would favor the wealthy, and poor people who could not afford protection would be left defenseless. The Icelandic system of law enforcement had a way to solve this problem by having transferable tort claims. If one did not want to seek damages himself, he could sell his tort claim to someone else, and that person would be able to seek damages on his behalf. Such a system allows those who are too weak or too poor to sell their torts to those who are more willing and able to seek justice on their behalf.

Suppose a victim had no heirs, would he have to watch a murderer get away scot-free? No. instead, a person was able to homestead the tort claim and seek justice on behalf of the murdered victim. Transferable tort claims allow those who lack friends and heirs to get justice done by strangers who, if lacking empathy, have a financial incentive to seek damages against others and punish violators.

One reason medieval Iceland avoided perpetual civil wars and open fighting was because people knew in advance who protected whom. People were also free to join associations that defended and collected tort claims on their behalf. It was in the self-interest of the members of the associations to defend people who were in their coalitions since both their reputation and their safety was dependent on making sure their members were protected.

During the three hundred years that Iceland lived in a state of anarchy, crime was relatively low. Rape and torture were uncommon and the killing of women was almost nonexistent. Friedman suggests that even during the worst fifty years of civil war that almost brought an end to the Icelandic system, the number of people killed on a per capita basis then was roughly equal to the current murder rate in the United States (Friedman 1979, 410). Thus, it is possible to have a system of law without a central coercive body without degenerating into the Hobbesian jungle. People use their customs and norms and codify them into law, and enforce them without perpetual open violence and without a nation-state. Medieval Iceland is not the only example where institutions developed protecting property and persons in the absence of a Nation-State.

The commercial law that exists today was not created by government, but arose privately. Commercial law arose in defiance of government. Merchants who wanted to trade internationally had to abide by countless government laws, making trading too complicated. There were also contradictory laws, making it difficult to conduct business outside of their own government's jurisdiction. Merchant law arose in order to have more uniform laws governing international trade. The market can provide diversity when it is necessary, like in the numerous types of deodorant brands that Bernie Sanders complains about, and uniformity when it is demanded, like in the case of video-cassette players all adapting to VHS over Betamax. In the case of international trade, what was needed were uniform laws, which governments were unable to provide. The market filled the void that government both caused and was unable to reconcile.

During the eleventh and twelfth centuries, there was a rapid expansion in agricultural activity. Due to the increases and expansion in technology and productivity, People could be fed with less human labor. This resulted in an increased demand for labor in other areas. The increased productivity of farming led to increased trade and a merchant class to better facilitate trade. Different languages, laws, customs, and geographic distances frequently impeded direct communication, making the trust necessary to engage in trade difficult. What was needed to engage in trust and trade was a market and law that acted as a *"language of interaction"* (Benson 1989, 646). Such commercial, private law that arose was not based on arbitrary rules, but largely based on Roman commercial law. However, much of the Roman law that was passed down through generations was not sufficient to meet the new problems that arose during the commercial revolution (Benson 1989, 647). This meant that the merchants themselves created the law that the merchants needed to better engage in commercial transactions.

Merchants developed their own court system for several reasons. Government courts would not honor any contract that involved paying interest since the royal courts considered interest a form of 'usury'. Government courts in one country would often refuse to uphold contracts made under the laws of another country, making international trade difficult. As Benson points out, *"common-law courts would not consider books of accounts as evidence, despite the fact that merchants held such records in high regard"* (Benson

1989, 650). Another reason for merchant courts is that the judges on state courts lacked the technical knowledge relevant to international trade. Since such judges and lawyers lacked the knowledge of how trading works, they would often enact highly complex and punitive laws which were more a hindrance than a help.

In order to make sure that the merchants from different regions would respect each other's decisions, the merchant law was developed to foster trust and reciprocity. Credit instruments were developed during this time in order to make trade easier. In order to ensure trust, fraud was forbidden. Part of reciprocity involved not favoring one side more than another. A contract that is heavily one sided, like the mystical social contract, is not considered a valid contract, since no person would voluntarily agree to a contract that imposed all the obligations on him while providing another party with all of the benefits. Merchants' notions of fairness and fraud were based on customs. Different merchants from different regions brought their customs and norms with them and through a process of trial, error, and competition, those customs that were shown to be the most efficient were adopted and those customs which were not beneficial to both parties were weeded out (Benson 1990, 32).

Rules of evidence and procedures were simplified, appeals were forbidden to avoid unnecessary delays, lengthy testimony under oath was avoided; debts were freely transferable through informal 'written obligatory,' a process developed by merchants to simplify the transfer of debts; actions by agents in transactions were considered valid without formal authority; and ownership transfers were recognized without physical delivery (Benson 1990, 34). All of these legal innovations were adopted by merchant courts to better facilitate trade and ensure trust.

To ensure that the merchant court decisions were fulfilled, boycotts and ostracism were used against merchants that refused to agree to the courts' verdict. Since merchant law required reciprocal arrangements to get voluntary agreement and to increase trust, the laws that developed were based on individual rights (Benson 1990, 36). The merchant laws form the basis of many of the laws of international exchange in use today.

Other examples of private law where government was either absent or unhelpful to protect property and individual rights include Celtic Irish law, which existed from around the 8th until the 17th century (Peden 1973) and the so-called 'Wild West'. Present day Zomia has remained stateless for over a thousand years, among other areas.

IV. Decentralized Self-Governance Among Heterogeneous Groups

Both medieval Iceland and the private creation of commercial law contradict the idea that law must be a creation of the state, or that a state is necessary to enforce the law. Gossip, sanctions, and being declared an outlaw are just some of the methods that have been utilized to get people to abide by verdicts that are not in their favor. One objection to a case such as medieval Iceland or merchant law is that such people are a homogenous group. While the merchants might have had different customs and likely spoke different languages, they were in the same profession and had the same goal in mind when the law was created. Medieval Iceland was populated by people with similar customs and backgrounds. So, perhaps the law can emerge without a monopolistic legal system among homogenous groups, but how about heterogeneous groups? How about groups which do not share similar values and who are mortal enemies of each other? Isn't a nation-state needed among them in order to make both groups get along? Peter Leeson has addressed this issue by looking at the decentralized system of criminal law among bitter enemies. Looking at how heterogeneous social groups who have antisocial feelings towards each other can nevertheless set up signals, incentives, and institutions to help reduce interpersonal violence provides some evidence about how there can be relative peace and freedom without the existence of a nation-state.

Between the 13th and 16th centuries, there were violent hostilities on opposite sides of the Anglo-Scottish border. Until the 17th century, the borderlands between England and Scotland were divided into six territories—called marches—three on each side. Neither England nor Scotland controlled the borderland since the laws of both Scotland and England applied to the territories, but not the border to cross them. Since neither government controlled the border, the border to cross either Scotland or England was anarchic (Leeson & Coyne 2012, 22). There was no state authority to create or enforce laws on the border or that dealt with cross-border crime (Leeson & Coyne 2012, 23). The lack of a government enforcing cross-border rules was especially problematic since Scotland and England were mortal enemies. They would engage in violence and individuals from each side would raid inhabitants on the opposite side of the border. This raiding involved murder, theft, arson, and whatever other violent means were necessary to destroy the inhabitants and their property. According to Leeson, *"frequent war left both border areas decimated, and inhabitants had little incentive to establish productive enterprises that would only be destroyed in the next violent outburst between their nations"* (Leeson 2009, 477). It would seem that both sides engaging in constant war proves Hobbes' prediction of anarchy right and that the remedy was a nation-state.

Fortunately, to prevent totally bloody war and chaos, the border inhabitants' interactions led to a decentralized system that gave rise to customary rules known as *"leges marchiarum"* or the law of the marches (Leeson 2009, 481). These rules developed based on cross-border interactions in order to deal with the problems of murder, plunder, and arson. Since the border inhabitants from opposite sides of the border hated each other, it wasn't realistic to create a cease-fire, but only to try to create rules to reduce the violence as much as possible. If a person was convicted of murdering another border inhabitant, the murderer was required to offer financial compensation or himself to the victim's family. The victim's heirs could either execute the murderer or ransom him to the murderer's family.

In order to enforce the law of the marches, the borders developed a court to settle cross-border disputes and punish violators (Leeson & Coyne 2012, 24). The court was composed of a jury of twelve men, six English and six Scottish. There was no nation-state to enforce the jury's verdict in order to ensure that the verdicts would be enforced. One way to get people accused of a crime to cooperate was to post bonds. The guilty party's family members were held as hostages in order to get them to comply with the verdict. If they didn't comply, their family members would be killed. (Leeson 2009, 491). While not the most civilized way to get people to appear in court and accept a verdict, it was superior to the open war that broke out previously in its absence.

Theft was considered a violation of the law of the marches and the punishment for theft was double the amount of damages. The *"two teeth for a tooth"* as Block often refers to it, was a part of common law and the law code of medieval Iceland, as well.

While the law of the marches did not totally eliminate violence, the decentralized Leges Marchiarum did reduce the hostilities that existed before such rules developed. The mere presence of such rules improved trust between the opposing factions by specifying which acts were considered legitimate and which were considered illegitimate and punishable. The day of truce also reduced the expected benefit of engaging in violence—by having to pay compensation—and reduced the cost of being victimized (Leeson 2009, 494). Even the Nation-State fails to completely eliminate violence. Reduction of violence is sufficient. Neither anarchic nor state societies are able to totally eliminate violence and bring peace.

V. Somalia Pre-Anarchy and Somalia Post-Government

A man walks up to an economist and asks him how his wife is doing. *"Compared to what?"*, the economist replies.

Utopia is not an option. The question is not which system is 100% perfect, but rather holding the maxim view, which system is more liberty-augmenting than the alternative. I have explained different examples of how legal institutions emerged without the existence of government; how social norms developed and how private institutions dealt with such norms; how law has existed in the absence of the state; how people were able to protect their property through restitution, and people ensured compliance through boycotts, developing good reputations, bonding; and in the case of violent feuds, holding people hostage in order to make a person accept his verdict. It is now necessary to compare and contrast anarchy with government. The mere demonstration that law has existed and could be enforced without being created by the state does not address the argument that a nation-state improves the protection of property rights, only that anarchist law is capable of existing.

One way to show that liberty is augmented without a government is to compare the same society with a government to that same society without one. Somalia from 1991-2005, when Somalia's nation-state dissolved, is a good case study to show that life under anarchy is preferable to life under a nation-state. Somalia's government collapsed in 1991. Rival groups immediately tried to plunge the country into a civil war in order to take over the reins of power and install a new government. The rival factions were unsuccessful in installing a new government after Siad Barre's dictatorship fell. In 2006, the Transitional Federal Government (TFG), which had been created in exile two years earlier, entered southern Somalia and tried to take over. Opposition to the TFG increased support for the Islamic Courts Union (ICU), which ended up installing itself as a government in some parts of Somalia. Later in the year, Ethiopia invaded Somalia, overthrew the ICU, and installed the TFG in the nation's capital (Powell, Ford, & Nowrasteh 2008, 657). Therefore, since Somalia ceased to lack a national government, starting in the end of 2006, Somalia could no longer be considered anarchist. Therefore, the years to judge Somalia are from when it was ruled by a government—from 1969-1991 and when Somalia's government was absent, from 1991-2005.

Most of the residents of Somalia during the time of Barre's rule were small farmers. The farmers had little influence in shaping the policies of the Somalian government and were constantly mistreated. Beginning in the 1970s, the state laws nationalized the land and water. Under the Somalian government, the only way to own land was to get permission from the state. In the 1980s, the land ceased to be nationalized and was "privatized" by being given to those with political clout. Most of the government's budget went to the military, while less than 1% went to social services (Powell, Ford, & Nowrasteh 2008, 659). Since the public sector failed to provide goods and services to the people, black markets arose to fill in the void. The black markets were able to provide healthcare, education, and investment credit to people.

After the Somalian government collapsed, there were improvements in overall living standards in many ways. Livestock trading increased enormously. The value of cattle sales increased 600% and the number of sales quadrupled from 1989-1998 (Powell, Ford, & Nowrasteh 2008, 660). The amount of trading in goats and sheep in Somaliland and Puntland was greater in 1999 than when under the national government (Powell, Ford, & Nowrasteh 2008, 660). Besides the pastoral sector, the commercial sector also increased under anarchist Somalia. Companies such as General Motors and Coca-Cola conduct business in Somalia and hire Somalians. Many international companies avoided doing business in a number of Africa's nation-states, so the fact that they decided to expand their companies and invest in Somalia was a good sign that property rights were more secure there (Powell, Ford, & Nowrasteh 2008, 661).

Comparing the last five years that Somalia had a state (1985-1990) to the last five years Somalia had anarchy (2000-2005) demonstrates that out of 18 development indicators, Somalia improved on thirteen of them, while only two—adult illiteracy and school enrollment declined

(Powell, Ford, & Nowrasteh 2008, 662). In areas such as life expectancy, infant mortality rate, extreme poverty, number of doctors, and percentage with access to food, water, sanitation, and healthcare, Somalia improved under anarchy compared to when it was ruled by politicians (Leeson 2007, 697).

Powell, Ford, and Nowrasteh (hereafter PFN) use the *World Development Indicators* to compare Somalia's performance under anarchy with 41 other sub-Saharan African countries (Powell, Ford, & Nowrasteh 2008, 662). This allows a comparison of anarchist Somalia with other countries ruled by governments on 13 variables, such as the death rate, infant mortality, and life expectancy. While Somalia is low compared to Western standards, it ranks in the top 50% of African nations in 5 of the 13 variables and near the bottom only in infant mortality, immunization rates, and access to improved water sources. Somalia as a nation-state ranked in the bottom 50% of all the seven variables available during the years 1985-1990 (Powell, Ford, & Nowrasteh 2008, 662). Life expectancy fell by two years from 1985-1990, but has increased for five years since becoming stateless. Only 3 of the 42 countries have improved that much since 1990. Sans state, Somalia's death rate has improved its ranking from 37th to 17th since 1990.

Since becoming stateless, Somalia has developed institutions that provide currency, defense, dispute-resolution, and laws that protect persons and property. In Somalia, a clan leader enforces the law based on customs. The clan leader is not a government since all adults are free to choose a clan leader whose verdicts they agree to abide by. Individuals are free to either start a new dispute-resolution insurance group themselves or join an already existing insurance group (Powell, Ford, & Nowrasteh 2008, 667). The Somali law is decentralized and is based on custom. The Somali customary law has existed since pre-colonial times and continued to operate under colonial rule and under anarchy. The Somalia nation-state tried to replace the customary law with government legislation and enforcement. As PFN point out, *"in rural areas and border regions where the Somali government lacked firm control, people continued to apply the common law. When the Somali government collapsed, much of the population returned to their traditional legal system"* (Powell, Ford, & Nowrasteh 2008, 666). While the nation-state tried to enforce its edicts, since the law did not arise organically, but based on norms and customs that people valued and respected, the government law failed to be enforced. Government legislation was considered inferior to decentralized, customary law, as it often is.

The Somalian legal system outlaws the usual: homicide, torture, rape, theft, extortion, and other violations of property and person. The legal system focuses more on restitution and making the victim whole than the inferior criminal law. The criminal law is more concerned with punishing the aggressor. Civil or customary law is more concerned with restitution. Much like the law of the marches mentioned earlier, according to Somalian law, an animal thief must return two animals for every one he stole (Powell, Ford, & Nowrasteh 2008, 667).

Somalia is far from a civilized, industrialized country and compared to Western governments it is lacking in freedom, but the purpose of showing how Somalia has improved under statelessness is not to paint a rosy picture of Somalia, but rather to see whether eliminating the government improves society. I am not presenting Somalia as a shining beacon of freedom, but rather as an example to show that life without a government does not result in worse violence and bloodshed than life under politicians. People are generally not suicidal creatures and if having a state is not an option, people will adapt to their environment and find alternative arrangements to protect themselves, to increase their living standards, and improve their lives and the lives of the people around them.

VI. Why Do Most Nations Fail and Why Has Exporting Democracy Abroad Failed?

The great economist Thomas Sowell once asked, not why are so many people poor, but why are so few able to become rich? For most people in the world, freedom is not the norm. The vast majority of the population does not have access to many of the things Western societies take for granted. If the nation-state is truly what leads to an increase in freedom, then why don't most nation-states exhibit these characteristics? As explained earlier, most nation-states are on the brink of collapse or in dire straits. Most nation-states have failed to provide the liberty and security they promise. Therefore, the question should not be that since some nation-states do not result in failure the solution is a nation-state, but why are some nation-states successful, while most are not? What determines how successful a nation-state will be?

While I am not so presumptuous as to have an answer for how to create a successful society, I do hope to provide some theories to possibly explain why exporting democracy has worked in some areas but not in others. Chris Coyne, Peter Leeson, and Boettke (hereafter CLB) have tried to explain what determines how successful the rule of law is and why the rule of law is respected and enforced in some areas and not in others. Borrowing a phrase from Ludwig von Mises, they have argued that the regression theorem determines the stickiness of institutions. Which institutions will stick and be successful depends on the institutions, norms, and culture of the previous time period. Or in their words, *"The regression theorem maintains that the stickiness, and therefore likely success, of any proposed institutional change is a function of that institution's status in relationship to indigenous agents in the previous time period"* (Boettke, Coyne, & Leeson 2008, 331). They argue that there are three different types of institutions: those imposed by a domestic government; those imposed by a foreign government; and those that emerge spontaneously as a result of individuals' actions, but are not formally designed (Boettke, Coyne, & Leeson 2008, 335). The institutions that are the stickiest emerge spontaneously. If a foreign or domestic government enforces rules that already subscribe to the endogenous institutions, they are successful. Those that try to impose their legislation from top-down are not. CLB mention that the reason that reconstruction in Japan and West Germany succeeded was because both German and Japanese culture had a positive view of trade, market exchange, and democracy. The reconstruction in Bosnia failed because the political climate and the climate of private individuals were not aligned. In Bosnia, there were numerous conflicting political interests and when democracy was trying to be exported from above, there was no effort to try to get people's interests to coincide. Different political institutions within the nation-state had different, and often conflicting constitutions. The timing of the elections was rushed before there was grassroots support. (Boettke, Coyne, & Leeson 2008, 349).

The reason why Poland had a successful transition from a communist dictatorship into a more capitalistic government than Russia was because before the collapse of communism in Poland, the Poland government passed the *"1988 Law on Economic Activity, which granted every Polish citizen the right to engage in private business"* (Boettke, Coyne, & Leeson 2008, 351). In Russia, the reformers decided to immediately privatize 70% of state enterprises before allowing a gradual transition, where the cultural climate was not in sync and capable of transitioning to a more capitalistic society. It isn't enough to privatize industries for capitalism to work. If the masses and the culture are not ready to adapt, one can't force freedom. Even when Poland was under communist rule, the Poland government allowed some private businesses to operate, where none were allowed under the Soviet Union. People in Poland have some experience with seeing private enterprise operate and were more open to it, allowing for a successful transition.

Lansing studied the Balinese water temples. The water temples across Bali were also considered places of worship for the various gods the people of Bali worshiped. In the

1970s, the International Rice Research Institute decided to usher in the "Green Revolution" for the citizens of Bali, which would get rid of the 'backwards' practices of rice production and replace it with rice that required fertilizer and pesticides. The government instituted this new policy by encouraging farmers to plant rice without taking account of the traditional irrigation schedule dictated by the gods. At first, there was a boom in rice production. But after a water shortage, there was an outbreak of rice pests and diseases (Boettke, Coyne, & Leeson 2008, 340). But the real problem was that the Balinese government failed to understand the implications of replacing having gods determine water irrigation with modern technology. Farmers did not understand the new system and could not adapt to the new innovations and institutions. Imposed governance often fails to be reciprocal since legislation is based on authoritarian edicts, whereas spontaneous law is a result of *"mutual benefit through exchange agreements"* (Benson 1991, 53).

The above discussion highlights the importance of ideology – and not the rule of law – in determining a successful society. In a superstitious society where private property is considered an enemy of the gods, private property rights are unlikely to be respected no matter which laws are passed. Many nation-states fail because government interests are at odds with the interests of the citizenry. Hayek distinguished between laws and legislation. Laws arise spontaneously and are not deliberately designed, whereas legislation is centrally created. Government legislation that goes against what people are used to is unlikely to be adaptable and successful. For the supporter of the Nation-State, this means that government's role is simply to enforce the law and not create it, or the role of government is simply to enforce preexisting laws which conform to cultural norms and expectations then the government's role is not to determine the rules of the game, but to enforce the rules which already exist. If a successful government's job is not to create rules, but to enforce them, this can also be done by private institutions. Citizens could pick their own defense agency and arbitrator instead of having one foisted on them. Furthermore, without a price mechanism, there is no way for those in government to determine if they are doing a good job or not. It is also not clear how those in government ascertain that they are satisfying the people without the people demonstrating this by showing them that their actions which are successful generate a profit and those which do not generate a loss.

VII. The Roving Bandit vs. The Stationary Bandit: A Justification for the Existence of a Nation-State

Ludwig von Mises explains that the problem with socialism is a lack of economic calculation. Without a pricing system there is no way to determine who should produce what, how much of it should be produced, and what is the most successful way to produce it. If one says that government should be limited to police, military, and courts, who determines how many policemen and courts there are, and how big the military should be? Who decides how much taxation is necessary and what incentive is there for government to eliminate waste or even be aware of it if it is not possible for them to be put out of business by a competitor who is less wasteful?

Holcombe argues that the government is not designed to provide goods and services but to redistribute wealth. The government is described as a stationary bandit that extracts income from people and in exchange removes the roving bandits who would be even more predatory (Holcombe 2004, 329). According to the stationary bandit model, law and order is a public good. Primitive societies where goods were held in common were able to protect themselves, but in agrarian, individualized societies where property was not held in common, there was little incentive to produce public goods, such as law and order. In a society of 1,000 people, a person only gets $1/1,000^{th}$ of the protection from producing law and order, so it would not be worth it to produce the public good himself (Klitgaard & Tinggard 2003, 256). Since there would be no protection for property, people were at the mercy of others who might rob them. A group of roving bandits, such as the Vikings from the 8th to the 11th century, would come along and rob a bunch of people in a village and then wander off. Since all of the gains would go to whoever was the strongest, it was worth it to engage in predation. In order to prevent such roving bandits from continually plundering people, the people would be willing to tolerate a stationary bandit instead. The stationary bandit would tax people, often heavily, and enforce and protect property rights. A roving bandit has a high time preference since he does not care that his stealing reduces the production incentives of the people he robs. On the other hand, a stationary bandit does not want to disincentivize the looted since he will also gain a share in the future of the looted produce. A stationary bandit has an incentive to take property from someone, but not enough to discourage him from no longer producing (the Laffer Curve). A stationary bandit also views roving bandits as competition and therefore has an incentive to prohibit roving bandits from pillaging his citizenry since that is his exclusive jurisdiction. A government is set up to act as a stationary bandit, which is less predatory than the roving bandit. A government prevents roving bandits from continually looting people and hence the people are better off under the stationary bandit than being under constant roving bandits that would take the whole produce instead of just a portion. According to Kintgaard and Tinngard, the state of medieval China has its origins as a stationary bandit, which they say the people preferred (Klitgaard & Tinggard 2003, 256).

While Holcombe does not make the assumption that law and order is a public good that won't be provided by the market, he does make the claim that in the absence of the state, the other alternative is to be at the mercy of even worse predatory gangs. The real choice is not between market or government provision of public goods, but between a roving gang or a stationary gang. In the absence of a nation-state, there would be a roving bandit who would be more predatory since he steals resources and moves along, without concern that doing so will cause his victims to produce less in the future. The government is like a shepherd who wants his animals to be nice and fat because he could sell them for more money on the market that way. Having free-range humans allows humans to be more productive than they would be under constant expropriation and slavery.

The stationary bandit theory has an overly pessimistic view of anarchy and an overly optimistic view of government. The theory assumes it is in the self-interest of the bandit to loot people and that other people would be at his mercy. As Benson, Friedman, and others have pointed out, under societies that lacked a nation-state, people would often join coalitions to come to their aid. Instead of one person defending himself against another, the coalition would come to help those who joined their group. The origins of Anglo-Saxton law had such a system. Anglo-Saxton law can be traced back to Germanic customary law (Curott & Stringham 2010, 10). Keep in mind that in an anarchist society, individuals would be free to keep and bear arms, which would allow them to adequately defend themselves from roving looters.

The Anglo-Saxons came from Germanic tribes that invaded England during the 5th century and brought their Germanic customs with them. Germanic customs had a legal code where people were part of tribes. Unlike a caste system, being in the tribes was voluntary. Each tribe consisted of a hundred men, called *pagi* (later to be known as "the hundred" in the 10th century), which was further divided into groups called *vici* who were responsible for policing (Curott & Stringham 2010, 10). The men who joined the tribes agreed to protect each other. While such tribes came about through custom and kinship, such tribal arrangements were later adopted by the English common law system during the 10th century. The hundreds were also divided into other groups, sometimes as small as ten men in a system known as *borh* (Curott & Stringham 2010, 11). Since there was no standing army or nationalized police force, groups such as the hundred acted as a decentralized police force. People who decided to join the groups took what was known as a *frankpledge*, which was an oath in which each group swore to both abide by the rules of the group and to protect the other members of the group when in need. In such a group, each member was responsible and looked out for the other members of the group. If one stole or committed other acts of aggression and failed to abide by the verdict, he was declared an outlaw. In order to ensure cooperation and trust, many members of the tribes refused to engage in trade and exchange unless a person was a part of the *surety* system. If a person was unable to prove that he was a member of a coalition that could pledge on his behalf, that conveyed a signal to people that such a person was untrustworthy, which caused him to have trouble joining another group for protection and engaging in trade and exchange (Liggio 1977, 273).

The Anglo-Saxon private legal system signals trust to people by trading with them, intermarrying with other groups, giving gifts, and having people vouch on their behalf. One solution out of the Hobbesian jungle is not to have to fight a roving gang on one's own but to join defense groups that would come to your aid if needed, like what occurred in Anglo-Saxon England.

Ayn Rand has opined that having different policing groups enforce different laws within the same geographical area would lead to violent conflict when the different policing groups would interact with each other and disagree on who the guilty party is and what the law should be (Rand 1964, 117). Under the law of the marches and medieval Iceland, peaceful resolutions were attained without government courts. In today's world, there are disputes between countries and disputes between people from different states. The solution to solve conflicts is not always an outbreak of violence. Such behavior is expensive and self-destructive.

VIII. A Theory on Why Private Agencies of Force Are Likely to Protect Property More Than Violate Property

Friedman asks the question: If both parties are unable to verbally communicate with each other, what determines how they interact? If two people are supposed to meet somewhere in NYC, but they haven't discussed where, Schelling says that people typically end up meeting at noon at Grand Central Station. They pick a known location and an obvious time which allows coordination without communication. Friedman's question is an attempt to explain that property rights are determined (and respected) based on people's strategic behavior, and solutions are developed even without communication. For example, suppose a dollar can be divided between two people, on the condition that both sides agree on how the dollar will be divided. Each person may have an incentive to want a larger share of the dollar. It is unlikely that a person will only accept 10 cents and allow the other person to keep 90 cents, and it's unlikely that a person wanting 90 cents of the dollar will believe the other person will agree to this. The likely result is that the dollar will be split in half since each person has an incentive to agree with how the dollar will be divided (in order to get it) and to maximize the amount he gets; a fifty-fifty split is the most likely scenario to ensure that both parties benefit as much as possible.

According to Friedman, peaceful resolutions regarding property rights are more likely to occur among people who have the same belief about property rights. Strategic behavior determines how property rights are respected or violated and using strategic behavior when it comes to interacting with each other is what makes civil society possible and not the existence of top-down legal systems. The use of strategic behavior to try to understand human behavior facilitates coexistence. A person is unlikely to give into a person's threats because it will increase bullying in the future. Conversely, a person is more likely to follow through on mutually agreed upon exchanges to foster a reputation of being able to deliver on his promises.

An example Friedman gives involves a person willing to chop down a tree that is blocking someone else's orchard in exchange for an apple. Why is it that a person wouldn't just steal the apple, but if after the agreement is reached the person who chopped down the tree would use force to get the apple if the apple owner failed to abide by his end of the deal? The reason is because people typically act based on other people's expectations. A person who just stole apples would be considered a thief and unjustified in taking that which doesn't belong to him. He would not only cause friction between him and the apple grower, but also any of the apple grower's friends or others who view theft as wrong. On the other hand, a person wants a reputation as not being a push-over, and because there are more people who consider it justified to take that which was promised to you after you have fulfilled your end of the bargain, a person is more likely to conform to such expectations. A person who took the apple by force only after being stiffed can say that he held up his end of the deal and he is not stealing the apple since it is now rightly his. He is able to find more people sympathetic to his situation now, which makes it more likely that the lumberjack would only take the apple by force after the apple orchard failed to act out his part of the deal. As Friedman mentions, while the lumberjack was just as capable of stealing the apple in either scenario, he has more of a reason to carry it out when the apple grower cheated him and the apple grower has less of a reason to resist. Such actions create a focal point that influences people's behavior in the future. The reason I will keep up my share of the bargain is to not only develop a reputation for honesty, but because I will get more backlash for failing to do so and have less people defend me when I commit fraud and fail to keep my promises.

Friedman mentions that if someone gets extorted for money, *"It is in my long-run interest not to back down because if I do I can expect further demands: 'if once you have paid him the danegeld/ You never get rid of the Dane.'"* (Friedman 1994, 8). If the roving bandit and the people in the village are around equally as strong, the people in the village are less apt to give in to the bullying since that tells the roving bandit that his bullying is successful and has a greater incentive to extort more in the future.

Friedman's main point is that rules that are enforced exist because they are both just and efficient. According to justice, each person owns himself. Having each person own the right to his body is not only just but is most efficient. It is easier for me to control the use of my body than someone else (Friedman 1994, 12). In a world without transaction costs, any initial allocation of property rights is efficient, but in the real world with transaction costs, the most efficient allocation of property is where I own me and you own you since it is easier to enforce such rules. By contrast, a society in which I own other people or everyone owns a portion of everyone else is not efficient. Rules tend to move in the direction that is at least locally efficient and that the rules that are most efficient (where people own themselves and what they homestead) and just are also the rules which tend to exist in society. So rather than having tension between what should be and what is, justice, efficiency, and the legal rules which exist complement each other.

The above explains how property rights, norms, customs, and laws emerge. The most successful laws are based on previous focal points. Customs and norms are not static or arbitrary but based on continuous interaction with people. The most successful interactions and behaviors are the ones that cause the norms to stick and get codified in law, as in the case of the common law. The common law was based on a case by case basis where whenever a conflict arose, the most efficient way to settle a dispute was the one which was written down for how to solve the dispute in the future. Through a process of trial and error, the norms that won out were those that were the most efficient at settling disputes by conforming to people's expectations. According to legal scholar Hasnas, the common law was not legislative law, but caused by case law. The law was about finding a result that both opposing parties found acceptable in order to resolve a dispute without violence having to be a solution (Hasnas 2008, 114).

When the basis of law is contractual law where the goal is mutual benefit and reciprocity, the rules which emerge are rules conforming to people's norms and expectations with each other. As shown above, these occur as a result of repeated interactions with others, not based on government edicts. The law was not created by government and can exist in its absence.

Suppose that instead of being provided by a nation-state, laws were provided by the market. It is likely to be the case that the law would be as Friedman predicts and has shown in the case of Medieval Iceland. The laws would prohibit murder, theft, and violence. People would contract out to a defense agency of their choice. If a dispute arose between a person contracted with Defense Agency A and Defense Agency B, it is unlikely that the court would be run by either agency but would find an impartial agency neither party contracted with in order to reach an impartial verdict. Both parties would agree to abide by the verdict and if one party did not, it is likely that he would be declared an outlaw, during Medieval Iceland, and during the Law of the Marches, and during the Law Merchant (as well as during the California Gold Rush, the Wild West, and during the 1,000 years of anarchy in Ireland. From the 8th century (possibly before) until the 17th century, Ireland was in a state of anarchy since there was no legislature, no bailiffs or police, and *"no trace of State administered Justice"* (Peden 1977, 83). Instead, Ireland had contractual law where people hired representatives to enforce contracts for them and joined in sureties for protection (Peden 19777, 86-87).

If the United States decided to go anarchy by having the state eliminate its taxing power and allowing competition, it is reasonable to assume that such private defense agencies would protect property to a greater degree than the government does. One major difference between the state and the market is that firms in the market are concerned with making a profit and successful firms would engage in behavior that would generate a profit. Would firms make more money by stealing and robbing from people and acting like a stationary bandit, or would they make a high profit by protecting people and their property?

The libertarian theory of property rights is homesteading, which is first come, first serve. The first person to be in contact with (and utilize) the land is the one who gets to claim ownership over it. The idea of homesteading is not an arbitrary theory of property, but a natural one.

Related to homesteading is the endowment effect. The endowment effect states that people value the good they possess more highly than a good they do not possess. The endowment effect creates a feeling of loss aversion where people are willing to spend more resources devoted to protecting their property than others would to seize theirs. Loss aversion is when a person is more sensitive to losses than gains (Gintis 2006, 2). Thaler explains an experiment showing the endowment effect in action. In the experiment, people were randomly assigned the role of seller, buyer, or chooser. The sellers were given a mug (that originally sold for $6 at the school store) and were asked whether they would be willing to sell the mug at prices ranging from $0.25 to $9.25. Choosers were asked to choose for each price between receiving the mug or that amount of money. The experiment revealed that the average buyer was willing to buy the mug for $2.87 and the average seller was willing to sell the mug for $7.12. Choosers acted similarly to buyers by being on average indifferent to getting the mug or receiving $3.12. What the experiment revealed is that the owners of the mug valued the mug at more than twice the amount as non-owners (Gintis 2006, 4). The experiment demonstrates that once a person is currently in possession of a product, he is willing to spend more money to keep it than someone who is not currently in possession of the product would spend to acquire it.

The endowment effect is not just an economic theory used in experiments, but a natural tendency among humans and animals. In one study, observers studied a group of 11 toddlers and 13 preschoolers to see how often a toddler or preschooler possessed an object and how often they took the object from others. The results found that success was strongly and equally related to both how strong the person was and prior possession. The observers also found that toddlers recognize possession as a basis for asserting control rights, but do not respect the same rights in others. The preschoolers, more than twice the age of the toddlers, use physical proximity both to justify their own claims and to respect the claims of others (Gintis 2006, 7). The endowment effect demonstrates that even very young children are willing to spend more energy defending what they own than they would to take items from others.

Stevens studied horses competing for water. The water was located in pools that would form after severe rains. What Stevens reported was that out of the 233 horses observed, 178 (80%) of the horses who were by the pool first were able to successfully ward off the horses that tried to take their spot away from them (Gintis 2006, 8). This finding indicates that even animals recognize the homesteading theory of property.

Using our knowledge of the endowment effect, it would not be unreasonable to conclude that people would be willing to spend more money to defend their property and their life than they would to rob or hurt other people. Since market defense agencies are in the business of making a profit, it seems likely that they would make a higher profit defending property and life than being hired as goons to steal from others. People are willing to spend more money to defend their rights than they are to violate others. Therefore, the market would tend to reward the most profit-maximizing firms, which would be those who only defended persons and property.

Similar to Friedman's example with the apple grower and the lumberjack, a focal point is more likely to occur that reflects people's expectations with each other. Even in primitive societies, the taking of an object currently in possession of another individual was rare (Gintis 2006, 8). Since most cultures and norms already have laws against theft, defense agencies that were able to fulfill people's expectations of preventing and punishing theft would be met with a good reputation, whereas agencies which looted from people would be viewed with condemnation, just like how the mafia is viewed today. Successful businesses depend on good reputations, and being fair promotes a better reputation than extorting people.

During the Anglo-Saxon era, people were part of a surety system where they were responsible for the other members. There is no reason to believe that a similar system would not form again. Under a polycentric legal system, people joined voluntary associations that would come to their aid. In a market, there would likely be insurance agencies where people would contract out and pay for crime insurance, similarly to how people pay for life and health insurance. Insurance agencies suffer from an adverse selection problem. People willing to spend the most on health insurance are likely to be people who are already sick or going to be shortly, which is why insurance companies have measures to reward people for being healthy and it's why they offer lower rates to people who voluntarily take precautions. So too, people who wish to spend the most amount of money on crime insurance tell the insurance company that such people are those most likely to commit crimes, since why would a person unlikely to commit crimes want to spend a lot on crime insurance? Therefore, in order to prevent this adverse selection problem, crime insurance companies would give lower rates for those who prove they are peaceful, have a good reputation, and signal to the insurance company that they aren't going to be committing a lot of crimes.

IX. People Living in Older States are Worse Off Than People Living in Newer States

Oana Borcan, Ola Olsson, and Louis Putterman (hereafter OBP) explore how state development and economic development interact with each other. They look at various nation-states, starting at 3500 BC, when the first state came into being until the present day. What they conclude is that *"very old states have the least developed economies whereas the richest countries have intermediate state history scores...Our inquiry is supported by the empirical observation that old states like Iraq, Turkey, and China are poorer today than younger states like Britain, Denmark, and Japan"* (Borcan, Olsson & Putterman 2015, 2 & 3). OBP also say that, *"The more peripheral regions, which were slower to develop state institutions, were furthermore less exposed by raids by roaming armies and to incursions by migrating people"* (Olsson 2015, 8). According to OBP, the reason for this *"reversal of fortune"* (Borcan, Olsson & Putterman 2015, 8) is because older states have access to more taxes and higher tax rates, and they therefore tend to become more exploitative and corrupt. According to OBP, older states are worse in terms of per capita income than intermediate states (Borcan, Olsson & Putterman 2015, 28). OBP say that intermediate states fare best, whereas younger and older states are the most backwards. OBP say that younger states don't have the ability to build a solid tax base to fund public goods and that older states tend to misuse tax revenue at the expense of the economy. According to OBP, Britain is the ideal age a state should be (Borcan, Olsson & Putterman 2015, 35).

OBP's study is important because it reveals that the older the state, the worse the economy. If government is necessary, then why are younger states better off than older states? Why are living standards higher in places when state rule is younger than places with older state rule? If a nation-state is necessary for a free society and augments overall liberty, then it would seem that people living in older states should be at least faring equally well to people living in younger states, but the opposite seems to be the case. If that is correct, then I would argue that the existence of the nation-state diminishes liberty those that are worst off are those who have been living under a nation-state the longest.

X. Conclusion

Western conceptions of government tend to be considered paragons of justice and freedom. However, the enhanced justice and freedom in the West was not brought about by the creation of the state, but rather, arose spontaneously as a reflection of collective social values and customs, practiced by individuals who demonstrated mutual respect for divergent practices.

While there have been periods of history with violence, the reduction was caused more by an increase in commerce and respect for property rights, which Pinker does mention are factors, then simply the existence of a nation-state. A government is composed of human beings. If the nation-state is a democracy, there is no reason to believe that people who would steal from people if given the chance would not vote for people to steal on their behalf. If people want to dominate others, it seems like a haven which puts certain people on a pedestal and does not subscribe to them the same standards of morality as the rest of us is more likely to be a recipe for disaster. The potential for misuse of power likely explains why the vast majority of nations are not paragons of freedom. Freedom exists when your neighbors respect your rights. Commerce tends to cultivate good relationships, which is probably one of the reasons the Nazis did not attack Switzerland. Much of the Western legal system derives from the common law, which was itself a privatized law system. There have been areas without a state where property has been defended and the concept of individual rights has existed. Even in the worst fifty years of war in Medieval Iceland, the homicide rate per capita was no more than the current homicide rate in the United States. During the Industrial Revolution, people couldn't rely on public policing, but instead had to use private security. Private law enforcement during the 17th and 18th centuries functioned adequately when it came to reducing crime (Koyama 2012, 5-6). When either a domestic or foreign government imposes rules that are not consistent with the norms, culture, and expectations of the people, the citizenry is harmed. There are areas with a lot of crime lacking a nation-state, and there are areas with a nation-State with high homicide rates per capita. What may matter more than the existence of a nation-state is the ideology of the masses of the population. If the masses of the population do not respect individual rights or appreciate how private property is essential to a free society, a government imposing a law without a change in ideology is not going to be sufficient. Focal points that provide coordination and the right incentives are what improve freedom and relationships, not politicians.

161

References

1) Benson, Bruce L. "The spontaneous evolution of commercial law." *Southern Economic Journal* (1989): 644-661.
2) Benson, Bruce L. *The enterprise of law: Justice without the state*. San Francisco: Pacific Research Institute for Public Policy, 1990.
3) Benson, Bruce L. "Reciprocal exchange as the basis for recognition of law: Examples from American history." *Journal of Libertarian Studies* 10.3 (1991): 53-82.
4) Boettke, Peter J., Christopher J. Coyne, and Peter T. Leeson. "Institutional stickiness and the new development economics." *American Journal of Economics and Sociology* 67.2 (2008): 331-358.
5) Borcan, Oana, Ola Olsson, and Louis Putterman. "State History and Economic Development: Evidence from Six Millennia." *Available at SSRN* 2464285 (2014).
6) Curott, Nicholas A., and Edward P. Stringham. "The rise of government law enforcement in England." *The Pursuit of Justice*. Palgrave Macmillan US, 2010. 19-36.
7) Friedman, David. "Private creation and enforcement of law: a historical case." *The Journal of Legal Studies* 8.2 (1979): 399-415.
8) Friedman, David. "A positive account of property rights." *Social Philosophy and Policy* 11.02 (1994): 1-16.
9) Foreign Policy and the Fund for Peace. 2015, "Fragile States Index." Available at: http://fsi.fundforpeace.org/rankings-2015
10) Fuller, Lon L. *The morality of law*. Vol. 152. Yale University Press, 1977.
11) Gintis, Herbert. "The evolution of private property." *Journal of Economic Behavior & Organization* 64.1 (2007): 1-16.
12) Hadfield, Gillian K., and Barry R. Weingast. "Law without the state." *Journal of Law and Courts* 1.1 (2013): 3-34.

13) Hannan, Daniel. *Inventing freedom: How the English-speaking peoples made the modern world.* Harper Collins, 2013.

14) Hasnas, John. "The obviousness of Anarchy." *Anarchism/Minarchism: Is a Government Part of a Free Country* (2008): 111–132.

15) Holcombe, Randall G. "Government: Unnecessary but inevitable." *Anarchy and the Law: The Political Economy Of Choice* 354 (2007).

16) Huemer, Michael. *The problem of political authority.* Palgrave Macmillan UK, 2013.

17) Klein, Daniel B. *Knowledge and Coordination: A Liberal Interpretation.* Oxford University Press, 2011.

18) Klein, Daniel B., and Michael J. Clark. "Direct and overall liberty: Areas and extent of disagreement." *Reason Papers* 32 (2010): 41–66.

19) Klein, Daniel B., and Michael J. Clark. "Direct and overall liberty: replies to Walter Block and Claudia Williamson." *Reason Papers* 34.2 (2012): 133–144.

20) Kurrild-Klitgaard, Peter, and Gert Tinggaard Svendsen. "Rational bandits: Plunder, public goods, and the Vikings." *Public Choice* 117.3-4 (2003): 255–272.

21) Koyama, Mark. "The law & economics of private prosecutions in industrial revolution England." *Public Choice* 159.1-2 (2014): 277–298.

22) Leeson, Peter T. "Better off stateless: Somalia before and after government collapse." *Journal of Comparative Economics* 35.4 (2007): 689–710.

23) Leeson, Peter T. "The laws of lawlessness." *The Journal of Legal Studies* 38.2 (2009): 471–503.

24) Leeson, Peter T., and Christopher J. Coyne. "Conflict-inhibiting norms." *Oxford handbook of the economics of peace and conflict. Oxford University Press, Oxford* (2012): 840–860.

25) Liggio, Leonard P. "The Transportation of Criminals: A Brief Politico-Economic History." *Assessing the Criminal: Restitution, Retribution, and the Legal Process* (1977).

26) Peden, Joseph R. "Property rights in Celtic Irish law." *Journal of Libertarian Studies* 1.2 (1977): 81–95.

27) Pinker, Steven. "Decline of violence: Taming the devil within us." *Nature* 478.7369 (2011): 309-311.

28) Powell, Benjamin, Ryan Ford, and Alex Nowrasteh. "Somalia after state collapse: Chaos or improvement?." *Journal of Economic Behavior & Organization* 67.3 (2008): 657-670.

29) Rand, Ayn. "The nature of government." *The Virtue of Selfishness* (1964): 111-119.

30) Roser, Max (2016), 'Homicides'. *Published online at OurWorldInData.org.* Retrieved from: https://ourworldindata.org/homicides.

31) de Wolf, Aschwin. "Make Money, Not War: Steven Pinker's" The Better Angels of Our Nature: Why Violence Has Declined"." *The Independent Review* 17.1 (2012): 127-149.

Daniel Rothschild

Social and Asocial Capital:
Social Embeddedness and Government Intervention

Abstract: How important is social capital for a market economy and what effect does government intervention have on social capital? By looking at how the market is embedded within an institutional framework that depends on certain norms, government intervention can distort certain signals and destroy the social capital necessary for a well-functioning market economy by channeling resources into unproductive anti-market activity. The following essay explores the various definitions of social capital and discusses how government intervention distorts social capital, networks, and norms, and provides a theory of when government intervention can lead to a pushback, reaffirming previous social norms instead of government leading to more and more government intervention.

JEL Codes: B53, P37, Z13

I. Introduction

Frederick Hayek made the distinction between law versus legislation (Hayek 1973, 2012), or formal rules and informal rules (Pildes 1996; Leeson and Coyne 2012; Posner 1998; and Benson 1993). Informal rules are the unintended, unwritten social norms of a society or community. Formal rules are the legislative rules that are created from the top-down.

Leeson and Coyne (2012) make a distinction between three types of rules:

1) Legislation, which describes rules intentionally created by a monopoly rule-making enforcer called the state, which determines the rules for everybody in the area the state claims authority over. Such legislation is not produced for profit (Leeson and Coyne 2012, 4)

2) Private rules, which are intentionally created rules produced for profit, must satisfy the consumer by passing the market test. Examples of private rules are club goods (Lesson and Coyne 2012, 15), such as homeowners associations. Like legislation, private rules are intentionally designed. Unlike legislation, private rules are produced for a profit, whereas legislative rules are not.

3) Social norms, or informal rules. Social norms are the unintended social rules that emerge spontaneously. They are a result of human action, but not human design.

Understanding the difference between private rules, "public" legislative rules, and social norms is important when talking about generating social capital and the effect each type of rule has on improving or destroying social capital.

There are many views on what constitutes social capital. Though many of the views conflict, the basic agreement on what constitutes social capital is that it is an investment people make in social relationships. The social norms that develop from such relationships have a durable network of mutual recognition in order to achieve certain ends that would not be possible without such investments.

Here are some of those views:

According to Pierre Bourdieu, social capital is the aggregate of resources that exists within a group by having a durable network of (more or less) institutionalized relationships of mutual recognition (Bourdieu 1985, 248). As Siisiainen mentions, for Bourdieu trust has no place in his concept of social capital (Siisiainen 2000, 21). Instead, Bourdieu was interested in the role of social capital in creating issues of stratification and conflict (Fine and Lapavitas 2004, 19).

Another view of what constitutes social capital is Robert Putnam's concept, which states that instead of social capital involving conflicts and power, social capital refers to different networks, norms, and social trust which exist to help increase cooperation for mutual benefit (Putnam 1995, 67). For Putnam, social capital is a resource located internally, and involves increasing levels of cooperation.

According to Westlund, social capital is defined as social, non-institutionalized networks that reflect the norms, values, and preferences of the people in the networks (Westlund 2003, 1). Westland defines institutions as the formal laws, such as legislative rules, and considers informal rules as non-institutionalized. For Westlund, only the informal rules, such as social norms, constitute social capital.

Adler and Kwon mention that there are essentially two views of social capital. One group, primarily sociologists such as Bourdieu and Landes, define social capital as *"a resource facilitating action by a focal actor, a resource that inheres in the social network tying that focal actor to other actors. This view...begins with the idea that the actions of individuals and groups can be greatly facilitated by their membership in social networks, specifically by their direct and indirect links to other actors in these networks"* (Adler and Kwon 2000, 90). For such people, social capital is a resource located in external linkages of the focal actor. Another view they mention is that social capital is a feature of internal linkages that characterize the structure of collective actors, such as groups, communities, and organizations. (Adler and Kwon 2000, 91). In other words, for some, trust and reciprocity is the element of social capital, while others view trust as the product of social capital (Ikeda 2008, 172).

For Coleman, unlike other forms of capital, social capital is usually a public or collective good, as opposed to being a form of private property (Coleman 1988). According to Burt, unlike financial, human, or economic capital, no singular individual has exclusive ownership rights to social capital (Burt 1992, 58). For Westlund and Bolton (2003), however, social capital is not genuinely a public good since it is possible for the network or club to exclude outsiders from accessing the network that provides the social capital. Such thinkers attribute capital to the good itself, where human capital is increasing the stock of skills embodied in the individual, whereas social capital is embodied within social relationships or networks among people.

For Bourdieu, social capital derives from economic capital (Bourdieu 1983, 252), in the sense that investments in social capital are done for the purposes of economic gain, whereas, both Solow (2000) and Arrow (2000) consider social capital a non-economic concept, therefore describing social capital as a form of capital is inaccurate and misleading. Arrow considers social capital non-economic since the motives of increasing one's social network are not done as a form of investment, but for its own sake. According to Arrow, investment in capital implies a *"deliberate sacrifice in the present for future benefit"* (Arrow 2000, 4). Whereas, any benefit that comes from social engagement is a consumption good, done for its own sake and not investing in the present in order to obtain more in the future.

As shown above, different scholars have different, and often conflicting, definitions for social capital. Some view social capital as productive and increasing trust, whereas others view social capital as being unproductive in many cases. Social capital can be used to increase levels of trust, whereas for others social capital can be used for anti-social purposes to create division and power struggles. For many, the disagreements and conflicting attributes that define social capital is evidence that the term social capital is misleading and meaningless (Fine and Lapavitas 2004, 26). As shown above, according to some, social capital is an internal resource within the network, whereas for others, social capital is external. According to Fine and Lapavitas, the term social capital is so broad as to include virtually everything, and that the term social capital conflates economy and society (Fine and Lapavitas 2004, 17)

As I will explain in more detail below, my definition is that social capital is an asset that is invested with the goal of increasing social interactions among people in order to attain greater income in the future. Social capital is investing in other people in order to create trust and reciprocity to lower transaction costs. This allows for an increase in trade, often without having to be dependent on strong ties, such as family, in order to obtain higher expected benefits in the future. Successful social capital leads to higher levels of social interactions, such as increased levels of trust and reciprocity. Unsuccessful social capital leads to lower levels of trust and reciprocity among people who interact with each other. Social capital consists of the norms of generalized reciprocity and networks of trust that emerge unplanned over time, where such capital can be used as a way to help promote entrepreneurial discovery (Ikeda 2008, 181).

In Section 2, I provide the definition(s) of capital within the Austrian tradition, as well as the various definitions of social capital according to the economics literature. I will then show how in order to be consistent with other forms of capital, social capital must be similar to the other forms of capital, such as financial and human capital.

In Section 3, I explain different instances of government intervention, especially in urbanization, and the effect such intervention has on social capital. In Section 4, I provide my own theory of the role social capital plays in determining how people are likely to respond to government intervention, as well as the role government intervention plays in altering or destroying social capital. Section 5 concludes.

2. Social Capital is both capital and social

According to Fukuyama (2001), the norms that constitute social capital must be social and lead to cooperation in groups. Successful norms are those that increase such virtues as trust, reciprocity, honesty, and peaceful coexistence. This is the social aspect of social capital.

Ludwig von Mises states that capital can't be separated from monetary calculation, and is only possible under a market economy with private ownership over the means of production (Mises 2008, 262). Mises defines capital as the sum of the monetary equivalent of all assets minus the sum of the monetary equivalent of all liabilities (Mises 2008, 262). For Lewin, capital goods refer to the physical goods, whereas capital is not physical but refers to the total value of all capital goods under consideration (Lewin 1996, 8). For Chalupnicek, while physical capital can be easily materialized in physical capital goods, human and social capital is not usually as observable since it's embedded within the people themselves. Human capital investment changes the property of one's mind through newly acquired knowledge. Social capital investment changes the properties of the minds of people in terms of their social relations and their expectations of other people's future conduct (Chalupnicek 2010, 1234).

Chalupnicek states that, *"social capital is an individual's (or private) asset and, like other forms of capital, it is created by investing scarce resources in the present to obtain certain benefits in the future"* (Chalupnicek 2010, 1234). Unlike other forms of capital which can be accumulated by the investor without having to interact with other people, the creation of social capital is an investment in other people and therefore requires at least two individuals interacting with each other. Obtaining capital is a result of saving in the present in order to achieve a higher income in the future. This applies to social capital as well.

As Chalupnicek points out, *"These resources are invested by Person A in Person B and constitute a claim of A on B that B will behave in a certain way in the future, and an obligation of B towards A to behave in this way"* (Chalupnicek 2010, 1235-1236). This social capital creates a sense of reciprocity and mutual recognition on the claim. Social capital is created only if both Persons A and B recognize the action of A as an investment. If Person B recognizes this obligation, social capital owned by A is created and lasts as long as B recognizes A's claim or until the capital is used by B reciprocating his obligation to A. If, on the other hand, Person A invested resources in Person B and B refuses to reciprocate, then the claim Person A invested in Person B is lost, and like other forms of capital, malinvestment occurs.

The type of social capital described by Chalupnicek is similar to the social capital described by Coleman. According to Coleman, social capital is described as an obligation Person B owes to Person A, guaranteed by B's trustworthiness. When A does B a favor, A creates an obligation on the part of B to repay later. Once B fulfills his obligation to A, the social capital is expended and A's stock of social capital is reduced to that degree (Coleman 1990, 306). Coleman mentions that when A does B a favor, social capital is created for A, but not for B. The more obligations A has owed to him at any time, all else being equal, the more value is A's stock of social capital (Ikeda 2008, 168-169).

As explained above, one view of social capital is that it is an individual's productive asset by investing scarce resources in the present in order to obtain greater expected benefits in the future. Productive social capital is where such investments pay off, and unproductive social capital is where such investments fail to pay off. For example: A man may invest in buying fancy suits and a nice meal for a woman on a date in the hopes that she reciprocates by giving him companionship in return for the nice meal. The investment could be defined as successful if the woman eats the meal and reciprocates with companionship. A failed investment could describe a case in which the woman eats the meal paid for by the man, but does not reciprocate by failing to give her date so much as a hug goodbye. Social capital creates feelings of reciprocity on one person based on the other person's previous actions. While the example doesn't have to be trading companionship in exchange for meals, it illustrates the way in which social interactions and capital are intertwined.

It is also important to emphasize the difference between consumption and capital. Capital is an investment resource while consumption is foregone in the present in order to obtain a greater benefit in the future. If one does a favor for another person or invests in resources, not as an investment to expect reciprocity in the future, but because such a person enjoys providing resources to another person for his own sake, then such expenditure of resources is not social capital, but a social consumption good. As Chalupnicek explains, if a parent invests in his child's education as a form of social capital with the expectation that the child will reciprocate in the future, such as paying for the parent's old age home, this is an example of social capital. If the parent pays for his child's education, not in hopes of being reciprocated, but as a form of altruism where the parent derives pleasure in seeing his child go to school, paying for schooling is not an example of social capital being used, but rather the same good—using resources to increase the education of one's child—now becomes a consumption good since there is no expectation of reciprocating (Chalupnicek 2010, 1240).

This insight is critical since what determines whether something is social capital or social consumption depends on the meaning the person involved attaches to the good or service, and not based on the physical characteristics of the good. Therefore if a person decides to join a social networking group as an end in itself, joining such a club is not an example of social capital. On the other hand, if a person joins a social networking group in order to bridge his social capital and strengthen his ties by making connections to those in the group in the hopes of getting a future job opportunity, joining such organizations is an example of social capital investment.

Ikeda agrees with Putnam's view of social capital, which is a good that is composed of "social networks and the norms of reciprocity and trustworthiness that arise from them" (Putnam 2000, 19). Ikeda mentions that social capital is a type of contextual knowledge since it is based on the set of understandings and meanings held in common by the individuals that compose an informal community based on a particular location or in an on-going relationship (Ikeda 2002, 232). Social capital consists of the ethical habits and reciprocal moral obligations internalized by each of the community's members. Therefore social capital is typically location-specific and like other forms of capital, changes over time, based on the evolving norms within the community. Ikeda mentions that social capital is considered capital because the social norms of trust and reciprocity increase the productivity of labor and other factors of production (Ikeda 2002, 233). Ikeda agrees with Coleman that unlike the other forms of capital, social capital can't be owned by a single person since social capital is based on the norms within the society and the circle of connections investing in the social capital, and not a particular individual thing or person.

According to Ikeda, social capital is similar to the function of money in 5 ways:

1) Both owe their existence to the relations and expectations among members of a network
2) Both significantly promote entrepreneurship and trade

3) Both depend for its existence on the unintended contributions of members
4) Both generate for each member a greater benefit than what she contributes where these benefits cannot be fully predicted in advance
5) Both are "emergent phenomena" (Ikeda 2008, 176). Unlike money, social capital is location-specific and can't be transported.

Borrowing from Lachmann's insight that the capital structure is heterogeneous and encourages entrepreneurs to make new creative opportunities, Chamlee-Wright considers social capital as a process of social learning, a process that reveals how knowledge is discovered and spreads throughout the community across time and how such knowledge is revealed by others within the community (Chamlee-Wright 2008, 43). For Carilli, Coyne, and Leeson just like the entrepreneur is the agent of change when it comes to economic capital by aligning heterogeneous capital goods into multi-specific uses, likewise, entrepreneurs in the social realm act to align and discover new combinations of social capital (Carilli, Coyne, and Leeson 2008, 210).

Unlike the neoclassical school of economics that portrays capital as a homogenous good, or the sociologists who typically view social interaction from the starting point of methodological collectivism, Austrian insights in how capital is heterogeneous and that knowledge is not static and given, but is a discovery process, sheds light on how to view social capital. Granovetter (1985) accuses sociologists of having an over-socialized view of man. Since sociologists think in terms of groups, they view agents' actions as being determined by the institutions around them. Sociologists view man as if he lacks free will and that the institutional structure determines how human beings act. Likewise, Granovetter views many economists, specifically of the neoclassical stripe, of having an under-socialized view of man, as if mankind is an atom who acts outside of a social context who views his acting within a vacuum without influencing the people around him.

According to Granovetter, both the under and over socialized view of mankind are inaccurate. While human beings are social creatures that are influenced by the norms and laws of their society, their actions are not determined by them (Boetkke and Storr 2002, 166). Human beings are not slaves to their environment who must act according to some script consistent with central planning, nor do they not care about the society around them. Rather a more realistic view of how human beings interact is that they care about other people, react and respond to social norms, have feelings of social obligations, but also have free will to refuse to conform to the rules around them or attempt to change the rules of the game. There is no reason to assume that human beings are not influenced by the society in which they live or that they must follow the rules unconditionally, as if norms and laws force people to act in a certain way, instead of more realistically influencing the way people act.

While Gravoetter is aware that action is embedded in social relations and that economic activity takes place within society, he understands that the direction of influence also runs in the other way—from the individual to the social context and from the economy to society (Boetkke and Storr 2002, 166). Gravoetter states, *"That business relations spill over into sociability and vice versa, especially among business elites is one of the best-documented facts in the sociological study of business"* (Gravoetter 1985, 495). For Gravoetter, *"economic institutions do not emerge automatically in response to economic needs. Rather they are constructed by individuals whose action is both facilitated and constrained by the structure and resources available in social networks in which they are embedded"* (Gravoetter 1992, 7).

As Lewis and Chamlee-Wright (2008); and Meadowcroft & Pennington (2008) point out, Gravoetter's distinction between weak and strong ties helps distinguish between the broad varieties of social capital. As Lewis and

Chamlee-Wright (2008) mention, bonding social capital involves the existence of strong social ties between relatively small homogeneous groups that share a common identity, such as families and religious organizations.

On the other hand, bridging social capital is found among weak ties and networks which have little in common and may even have a different moral code and social norms. As Lewis and Chamlee-Wright state, *"Bridging social capital allows people from different parts of the social structure to cooperate and share resources and thus is often the source of social change"* (Lewis and Chamlee-Wright 2008, 110). Bridging social capital describes networks that link acquaintances among different types of people, such as between a businessman and his customers (Madowcroft and Pennington 2008, 121). With bonding social capital and strong ties, since the people within the group share a common kinship, identity, or moral code, it is not as necessary to invest as much in market activity, which enhances the level of trust, as it is between people with weak ties who have little reason to trust one another. The market economy allows for a bridging of social capital so that people with weak ties can trust one another in order to engage in exchange.

A family has a level of trust, love, and kinship, and therefore doesn't need to rely on market signals in order to interact and engage in exchange with one another. The pricing system serves as a signal in order to get people with weak ties to trust one another more and engage in economic exchange. According to Adam Smith, *"It is not from the benevolence of the butcher, the brewer, or the baker, that we expect our dinner, but from their regard to their own interest"* (Smith 1976, 26-27).

Mises viewed the market economy as being directed by the consumers, whom he describes as, *"callous and cold-hearted, without consideration for other people"* (Mises 2008, 270). The pricing system can be thought of as a form of social capital that strengthens weak ties, where strangers are able to trade with each other since the ability to exit from relationships with those who appear undeserving of trust and to enter new relationships with those who signal that they are more deserving strengthens market interactions (Meadowcroft and Pennington 2008, 126). Meadowcroft and Pennington also mention that social capital can be used to show trust, in the forms of brand name goods and money-back guarantees. These are forms of social capital that are created in order to signal trust and assurance to people. Private certification from a trusting company is another way different networks can signal trust to those whom they interact and do business with.

As shown above, social capital takes on many forms. Social capital can perhaps best be defined as how Chalupnicek viewed it, which is that social capital is an asset that is invested with the goal of increasing social interactions among people in order to earn greater income in the future. Social capital is investing in other people in order to create feelings of trust and reciprocity to lower transaction costs, allowing for an increase in trade, often without having to be dependent on strong ties such as family in order to obtain higher expected benefits in the future. Successful social capital leads to higher levels of social interactions, such as increased levels of trust and reciprocity. Unsuccessful social capital leads to lower levels of trust and reciprocity among people who interact with each other. Social capital is both *social* in that it improves social behaviors, such as trust, reciprocity, and honesty, and is *capital* in terms of being used as an investment to increase one's living standards.

It should also be added that social capital involves socialization with all people involved in the interactions. In other words, any type of social capital that leads to an increase in anti-social behavior among the participants (both the investor and those who acknowledge their obligation to reciprocate) is not successful social capital in any meaningful sense. Human capital, while different from social capital, involves a human increasing his marketing ability and sphere of knowledge as an investment to obtain greater income in the future. If someone believed that the way to obtain greater income for himself in the future is by committing suicide, such an action would be an example of unsuccessful human capital in action. A person is unable to generate an increase in future income for himself if he is dead. Therefore, any action which removes the human from human capital would be considered to be unproductive. Likewise, any investment which removes the social aspect from social capital would be unproductive as well.

3. How Government Intervention Leads To Changes In Social Capital

As mentioned earlier, there are both legal rules and social norms that influence the way people act. Chris Coyne, Peter Leeson and Boettke (hereafter CLB) have tried to explain what determines the success of rule of law and why it is respected and enforced in some areas and not in others. Borrowing a phrase from Ludwig von Mises, they have argued that the regression theorem determines the stickiness of institutions. Which institutions will stick and be successful depends on the institutions, norms, and culture of the previous time period. Or in their words, "*The regression theorem maintains that the stickiness, and therefore likely success, of any proposed institutional change is a function of that institution's status in relationship to indigenous agents in the previous time period*" (Boettke, Coyne, & Leeson 2008, 331).

CLB argues that there are three different types of institutions: those imposed by a domestic government; those imposed by a foreign government; and those that emerge spontaneously as a result of individuals' actions, but are not formally designed (Boettke, Coyne, & Leeson 2008, 335). The institutions that are the stickiest emerge spontaneously. If a foreign or domestic government enforces rules that already subscribe to the endogenous institutions, they are successful, while those imposed by legislation from top-down are not. CLB mention that the reason that reconstruction in Japan and West Germany succeeded was because both German and Japanese culture had a positive view of trade, market exchange, and democracy. In contrast, the reconstruction in Bosnia failed because the political climate and the climate of private individuals were not aligned. In Bosnia, there were numerous conflicting political interests and when democracy was being imported, there was no effort to try to get people's interests to coincide. Different political institutions within the nation-state had different, and often conflicting, constitutions. The timing of the elections was rushed before there was grassroots support. (Boettke, Coyne, & Leeson 2008, 349).

Coyne (2005) states that societies with successful transitions to a more free-market economy after post-conflict reconstruction are those with a shared ethic and ideology. Adequate horizontal ties or bridging social capital must exist as a necessary step for successful reconstruction. Countries with low levels of bridging social capital will be harder to successfully reconstruct and will have a lower probability of success compared with countries that have a higher level of bridging social capital (Coyne 2005, 10).

Coyne provides a theory of cultural change, known as "herding". People make decisions based on their access to both private and public information. A cascade occurs when an increasing number of individuals choose a certain course of action, where the level of public information increases (Coyne 2005, 11). What matters most for a change in ideology are the first movers who get the ball rolling. The masses do not simply believe the news or information that is given to them, but rather accept and adopt views by opinion molders and leaders whom they trust and have well-established reputations. Investing in social capital to obtain greater levels of trust and be perceived as a reliable opinion molder is an important investment for those who are interested in changing the minds of the masses. According to Coyne, the more connected the society, the higher levels of bridging social capital, the greater the potential for higher levels of cascades and a successful change in reconstruction (Coyne 2005, 14). One way that leads to influencing opinion leaders is for those in political power to subsidize certain media outlets and intellectuals.

Coyne mentions that if the population is easily able to receive outside information from the occupying forces, government efforts that engage in censorship will be easily recognized as such, making such censorship counterproductive (Coyne 2005, 18). The way to determine the prospects of success for changing opinions is to look at the political, economic, and social history of the society. Countries with lower levels of trust and a history of lacking economic liberalism will not be as successful in transition when compared to societies with greater levels of trust and more economic freedom (Coyne 2005; Pejovich 1999; Berggren and Jordahl 2005; and Campbell, Fayman and Heriot 2011).

Leeson (2005, 2007) and Carilli, Coyne, and Leeson (2008) point out how individuals interact and invest in social capital to send certain signals to people so they can convey their credibility and trustworthiness to others (Carilli, Coyne, and Leeson 2008, 211). The type of signals may be gifting, learning another person's language, intermarrying, or adopting another person's cultural practices (Leeson 2008).

As pointed out earlier, social capital is not static or fixed. Rather, social capital is more accurately understood as a continually changing and ongoing discovery process, where new forms of social capital are discovered and others are discarded when they no longer serve as an effective signal (Carilli, Coyne, and Leeson 2008, 211). Carilli, Coyne, and Leeson mention that before legal reforms in the credit market, the informal market signaled trust between borrowers and lenders, such as borrowers incurring the cost of building a reputation to signal to lenders that they are unlikely to default (Carilli, Coyne, and Leeson 2008, 214). Likewise, lenders signaled to borrowers that they are trustworthy by helping them during times of economic downturns. That helps borrowers be more economically productive and encourages borrowers to request more credit from them in the future.

By having the government intervene to create homogeneity, (for example making membership in a social network compulsory) the memberships' information signals cease to convey any information about the member's credibility (Chalupnicek and Dvorak 2009, 370). Leeson (2005, 2007) and Carilli, Coyne, and Leeson (2008) mention how government can create artificial trust, such as by the FDIC being the lender of last resort by backing up all banks in case of default. The government could also create artificial distrust, such as reducing the number of market interactions that occur because agents can't determine which signal is really conveying trust and which is artificially trustworthy as a result of government "guarantees."

Knowledge is dispersed and ripples throughout society. All of human knowledge is not in one head. If everyone had equal access to knowledge, and there was no such thing as asymmetric information, human beings would never be wrong. If they somehow made a mistake, everyone would know. A firm suffers losses as a result of an error in interpretation and judgment. When a firm expects to make profits but ends up suffering losses, it generally comprises an error in judgment. A firm's judgment turns out to be successful when it makes profits. The pricing system serves as knowledge surrogates, revealing information to people that relative prices have changed (Hayek 1945). That knowledge does not have to be intentional, but based on the circumstances of time and place. Profits signal that one has satisfied the wishes of the consumer; losses signal a failure to adequately do so. Such signals are a form of social capital that increases people's ability to access knowledge that they would not be able to discover otherwise. Social capital and the informal rules (and private rules) that occur in society are a result of trial and error, competition, and continuous interaction with people.

Social norms are an evolutionary process, based on continuous interaction with people. The social norms that stick are those that have shown to serve as successful signals that coordinate successful interactions among people. Because the rules are not imposed from above, but result from continual bargaining, the rules or social norms that end up being created are those that have shown to prove successful at generating reciprocity. As Benson (1993, 2001) points out, the evolution of customary law and commercial law arose as a way to settle disputes where the goal was not for one party to impose their will on another, as in the case of authoritarian law, but created to recognize reciprocity. The merchant law was created in order to facilitate trade, where the rules which developed were based on the different norms of the merchants. The law that was created from that increased trust and reciprocity, where the merchant law acted as the "language of interaction" (Benson 1989, 646).

What distinguishes government from the market is that government intervention are rules imposed from above, where one party asserts their preferences on another party who may not agree. Government intervention ignores the important insight that knowledge is a discovery process and is more than simple information. While the economics literature is replete with the concept of asymmetric information, what often seems to be ignored is the concept of asymmetric interpretation (Klein 2002; Klein 2012). Two people can see the same piece of information and have two different interpretations about the same event. What one person sees as a flaw, another might see as a benefit. In order for there to be an increase in social capital, there must be the freedom for entrepreneurs to engage in the discovery process needed to look at their local conditions and either act consistent with the norms and generate profit opportunities consistent with the recognized norms of society or act as norm entrepreneurs who attempt to change the rules of the game. Such successful rules are only possible in the absence of coercion. The way to see what people desire is to let them be free to choose. If I coerce a woman to marry me, that is probably a good sign she doesn't value marrying me, and even if she does, the only way to confirm this for sure is to see how she acts in the absence of coercion.

Echoing Mises' insight that socialism is not possible without a pricing mechanism and private ownership over the means of production, I would argue that there is no way to know which government-imposed rules are beneficial because government laws are not produced for profit by willing consumers. Therefore, any government intervention will lead to a destruction of social capital by violating the wishes of those within a community and imposing its own legislative laws onto those who may not agree.

Ikeda (2004) mentions that according to the theory of interventionism, the use of political power to intervene in the market economy leads to outcomes that differ from the intended or stated intentions. *"These perverse outcomes arise from the attempt to deliberately reconstruct spontaneously formed social orders, such as cities, or to consciously redirect spontaneous entrepreneurial-competitive processes. Owing to their incomplete knowledge and ideological predispositions, however, public choosers...fail to recognize that the source of such outcomes is inherent in the nature of interventionism"* (Ikeda 2004, 248).

There are numerous ways that government intervention affects social capital. As Hayek (1972) mentions, government intervention leads to a psychological change in the character of the people. According to Hayek, such a psychological change is necessarily a slow affair that can take many years or even generations to take effect. Since government ultimately relies on public support and opinion, the norm within society is that the state is acting legitimately, for if most people did not view state actions as legitimate, they would be met with resistance. For example, many people believe that if something is illegal, such an act is immoral. When politicians prohibit certain activities, even if the norm in society was not to view such actions as immoral, such illegal activity would be met with moral disapproval over time.

A few examples help clarify: It is currently legal in many states to sell one's blood, yet it is currently illegal to sell one's kidney. Many people in society view selling kidneys with greater disapproval than selling blood. Alcohol, while more dangerous than marijuana and psychedelic drugs, is both legal and met with greater moral approval than certain drugs which are illegal but less dangerous. An example Dan Kahan gives is cigarettes. Until around 1964, there were virtually no laws regulating cigarettes, and smoking was considered a sign of "sophistication and virility." Today, government intervention through sin taxes on cigarettes, as well as prohibiting public smoking, have caused smoking to be considered a disgusting habit that onlookers should not be expected to tolerate (Kahan 2000, 626).

Government intervention can create or increase hostility between cohorts. As Meadowncroft and Pennington mention, since there are people within a society with different moral codes, attempts to use the "power of the state" to impose a shared set of values or goals is likely to produce conflict, as different groups compete for the ability to impose their version of the "common good" (Meadowcroft and Pennington 2008, 124). Since different special interest groups attempt to use the state to impose their version of what is good onto those who may disagree, such government intervention is liable to destroy social capital and create more hostility by pitting people against each other.

Ikeda mentions that the very act of government intervention unintentionally weakens the moral aversion or psychological resistance people may have towards interventionism and therefore encourages more interventionism (Ikeda 1997, 176). The repeated use of coercion and compulsion—the political means—to solve a social problem causes people to grow accustomed to the idea that the way to solve a problem is through the state - the apparatus of coercion and compulsion - instead of through civil society or the market. Therefore, the act of government intervention creates an ideological change within the society; the ideology being that government is the way to solve problems. Ikeda mentions Nathan Glazer, who said that government interventionism breaks down what Glazer refers to as the "fine structure of society" by encouraging people to depend on government for help instead of traditional structures, like voluntary charity (Glazer 1988, 7).

According to Glazer, the reason for an increase in the welfare state and social programs is because the ethic of not having government redistribute wealth has been destroyed with ever-increasing acts of government intervention; people have become accustomed to government redistribution. According to Glazer, once government provides a service to people, such as taxpayer-funded welfare for the poor, there is a *"revolution of rising expectations [in which] we become ever more sensitive to smaller and smaller degrees of inequality"* (Glazer 1988, 4).

Charles Murray mentions that there was a radical shift in the view towards social welfare policy during the 1960s. Before the 1960s, social welfare policy erred on the side of caution by denying taxpayer funds to those who truly needed it in order to discourage those who didn't need government help from taking advantage of it. Now this assumption has been weakened, and the standard on who is able to be on welfare has gradually broadened (Murray 1984, 212).

Government intervention creates winners and losers. The winners are those who are able to successfully have the government intervene on their behalf, whereas the losers are the ones who are forced to pay for such interventionism. Ikeda (1997, 2005) mentions that government intervention encourages people who may have previously had an ideological aversion against using the government to obtain resources to advocate for government intervention to protect their property or re-redistribute their property back to them.

Government intervention leads to bureaucratic rules and red tape, such as in the case of regulation, as opposed to market discovery when it comes to improving consumer satisfaction. Making certain acts mandatory takes the fun out of the activity, crowding out the private resources that previously existed before the government intervention (Ikeda 1997, 252). Before the welfare state, there was a level of charity, which has now been crowded out by the state. As a result of government intervention, the moral gratification that comes from voluntary giving towards the deserving poor as well as gratitude from the recipients, , has turned benefactors into disgruntled taxpayers, and recipients into ingrates who feel they are entitled and have a right to the income of others (Glazer 1988, 129-131).

Gruber and Hungerman (2007) looked at how faith-based charity from churches were crowded out during the Great Depression as a result of FDR's New Deal. Gruber and Hungerman mention that the states that saw a large rise in New Deal spending on government transfers saw a decrease in private charity donations (Gruber and Hungerman 2007, 1064). The crowding out caused by government interventionism has been as much as 30% of church spending towards helping the poor (Gruber and Hungerman 2007, 1064). Once there is an expectation that government is going to "help" those in need, private organizations feel less of a need to help those in need.

Jane Jacobs (1961) mentions that determining which neighborhoods, cities, and streets are safe depends on the social capital of trust, which is generated not by public policing, but by members of the community "social policing" (Pildes 2002, 2062). Successful neighborhood policing is conducted by community members who have a specific stake in the safety of the streets, such as shopkeepers and those who walk down the street to shop, gossip, and watch others (Pildes 2002, 2062). As Pildes mentions, the informal enforcement of norms doesn't take place among a close-knit, homogenous groups, therefores such spontaneous voluntary policing is an example of strengthening weak ties by bridging social capital, as opposed to the strong ties of the bonding social capital of a homogenous group. Such voluntary eyes on the street are a result not of intentional formal rules, but of voluntary, unconscious, social informal rules and norms.

Ikeda (2004, 254) and (Pildes 2002, 2067) state the 4 conditions of street interactions that generate norms of informal social (as opposed to formal, governmental) policing that Jane Jacobs describes:

1) The public streets should attract people to the street, such as using the street to shop, thereby drawing a large crowd,

2) There should be short blocks with numerous opportunities to turn corners in order for people to vary their routes, thus making streets more interesting. Such short blocks allow for multiple meeting places, which increases one's exposure to their environment and allows for making unexpected connections,

3) The owners of the shops must have an interest in policing the street, as well as attracting numerous types of people to the street, so the streets are filled with many people who are "eyes on the street," some of whom are watching and some of whom are being watched. In other words, there should be a dense concentration of people, which promotes safety,

4) In the district, there should be a mix of new buildings and older buildings with lower property values, so that new ideas are less costly to develop.

These four conditions allow an increased level of trust to emerge, where "eyes on the street" allow for voluntary policing (Ikeda 2004, 254). In other words, the public spaces should be of interest to those who live, work, and shop there, and the inhabitants must have local knowledge in order to have a support network, so people walking down the street feel confident that they are safe. As Jacobs mentions, having a densely populated area that attracts people to the street allows eyes watching people and also increases levels of trust because people on the street interact with each other, such as a shopkeeper and his customers.

Ikeda (2004) points out how the networks of trust depend

on people able to communicate with each other and having a local community, which voluntarily attracts people to the neighborhood, allowing for people to interact with each other, increasing trust. Such great cities are an example of spontaneous order, which allows for self-regulation and self-policing without the need for central planning (Ikeda 2004, 256) by city planners. As Jacob argues, city planning destroys the social norms and social capital of trust that is created because they fail to understand how the social norms serve as a control for keeping the streets safe. Pildes (2002) and Ikeda (2004) point out that what allows for an increase in social capital (increasing trust) are face-to-face interactions with people, where new opportunities, friendships, and bonds can develop. City planners are under the mistaken idea that people want peace and quiet and so government intervention, as basic as widening a street, can destroy social capital. Widening a street in a crowded city means narrowing the sidewalks (Ikeda 2004, 258).

Sidewalks that are too narrow reduce social interactions among strangers and the networking institutions that depend on them. Widening the streets makes it harder for people to interact with each other, reducing the levels of trust as a result of government trying to make the community more spread out. Government interventions, such as zoning laws, also increase the price of rent in the community, attracting less diverse people and reducing the number of shops, because zoning laws artificially inflate the price of constructing a shop, making it less profitable. Such urban sprawl occurs as a result of government trying to widen the street.

As Pildes points out, redevelopment projects—based on the mistaken assumption by city planners that peace and quiet are preferable to a more dense population—were built away from the street, making it harder for people to congregate. This resulted in greater personal intrusion because people had to be invited to neighbors' homes for a cup of coffee, for example, since there were no other public places for people to meet and interact (Pildes 2002, 2068). The result of such government intervention led to people choosing not to interact with their neighbors at all, diminishing the levels of trust that would have existed had government not spread people out, making it harder for them to interact with each other (Pildes 2002, 2068).

It's important to point out a few reasons why government intervention fails to produce the desired results and destroys or reduces the social capital—the informal social rules and norms, networks which increase levels of trust and reciprocity— which government interventionists claim to promote. Much of the social norms which exist are a result of social learning and discovery. There are limits to people's knowledge; there are going to be unintended consequences that central planners are unaware of.

As Mark Pennington (2004) points out, it is not the case that people in the market are aware of the results of all their actions while those in government are not. Rather, both those in the market and those in government lack perfect knowledge. The main difference, however, is that government top-down intervention is centrally planned, where legislatures are unable to discover the errors that their central planning creates. Pennington mentions that the competitive market process acts as an inter-subjective discovery procedure, where contradictory ideas are constantly tested against one another. Entrepreneurs don't start from the position of knowing which goods to produce, how to produce them, in what quantities, and at what price to produce them, but acquire such knowledge over time. Likewise, consumers do not start from the position of knowing what they want, but are constantly changing their preferences in light of changing offers which are continually presented by competing entrepreneurs (Pennington 2004, 218). A discovery process is created through competition, where profit and loss spread information about which courses of action are more (or less) successful. It is profit and loss which signal indicators of which actions are valued by the people whom they interact with. The market has a mechanism to deal with radical uncertainty: revealing to firms that their actions generated a profit and were successful at satisfying the consumer. Without profit and loss and without private ownership over the means of production, there would be no way for market participants to improve the lives of those they interact with or know that the course of action they took was the right one. The government, by contrast, does not operate on profit and loss, and therefore, there is no mechanism in place which signals to those in government that their intervention created the desired result. Since government lacks the signal that acts as a knowledge surrogate, there is no way to know that the course of action the interveners took was the right one.

Another example: Unlike government regulatory bodies which lack both the technical and local knowledge and a pricing mechanism in order to determine whether such regulation passes the market test, for-profit competitors have a strong incentive to reveal the shadiness of other firms. Regulatory bodies are more likely to be captured by the industry and be susceptible to bribes. As Klein (1998, 548) points out, those in the market for assurance in order to signal their trustworthiness to others have an incentive to broadcast not only evidence of their trustworthiness, but also evidence of their competitors' lack of trustworthiness. They do so by making rival claims in their advertising, promotions, and marketing (Klein 1998, 548). As Klein states, *"of the 65 advertising claims resolved by the Better Business Bureau's National Advertising Division in 1992, almost all of which dealt with the truth or accuracy of advertising claims, 47 were brought by competitors"* (Klein 1992, 548). Such safety assurance can only come about through a process of discovery, competition, trial, and error that depends on the local knowledge and circumstances of time and place. As Wildavsky points out, *"Safety results from a process of discovery. Attempting to short-circuit this competitive, evolutionary, trial and error process by wishing the end—safety—without providing the means—decentralized search—is bound to be self-defeating"* (Wildavsky 1988, 228).

4. A Theory of When Government Intervention Can Lead to More Government Interventionism and When It Can Lead to a Reduction of Government Interventionism

What is missing from this conversation concerning social capital and government intervention is an explanation of how government intervention can lead to a reduction in government legislation and the power of the state. While Coyne, Leeson, and Boetkke have provided a theory of why certain economies are able to successfully transition towards a market system and away from greater government control, what is missing is a theory explaining what causes governments to reduce the amount of intervention in the economy.

Higgs (1987) mentions that government intervention increases during periods of crisis. Even after certain wartime price fixing and controls, the size of government never reduces back to where it was before the state intervened in the economy, creating what Higgs calls the 'ratchet effect'. What is missing is a theory for the periods during which government reduces interventionism in the economy. If Higgs is correct that real or perceived crises cause the government to grow, what causes (at least in certain areas), government intervention to decrease? It is this question that I will attempt to explore.

The role and size of the state ultimately rests on public opinion. If public opinion states that government intervention in the economy is necessary to make people feel safer, there is going to be more support for government programs that create a feeling of safety. If public opinion felt that government intervention made people less safe, there would be fewer government programs related to public safety. It is the meaning that people attach to events that ultimately determines how they are perceived and interpreted. The facts never simply speak for themselves. If an act of government intervention is perceived as protecting the public and helping the poor, there is likely to be less resistance than if a piece of government legislation creates a perception of government violating the norms of society and acting outside its boundaries. If government intervention violates the norms of reciprocity and is perceived as such, such government interventions are liable to provoke greater resistance than if an act of government intervention is seen as conforming to their societal expectations, as perceived by public opinion.

Louis Kaplow (1986) argues that while the government has traditionally been seen to have an obligation to compensate for the harms it causes on innocent private property owners (such as paying fair market value for homes the government takes in the case of eminent domain), government should violate such norms by refraining from compensating the victims of homes that the state takes for "public benefit." The societal norm that government has an obligation to compensate people for homes it takes is codified in constitutional provisions, such as the Takings Clause and the Contracts Clause (Louis Kalow, 1986).

The justification behind Kaplow's support of government violating the norms of reciprocity by failing to reimburse homes it seizes is to reduce the number of instances of eminent domain.

Pildes explains the reasoning behind Kaplow's view in terms of the importance of social capital—being defined as following the social norm of reciprocity— influencing people's support for government policies. According to Pildes, there is a perception among the public that behind the support of "the social contract" is the idea that each person is required to sacrifice roughly proportional to the sacrifice of others (the progressive criticism of the rich not paying their fair share of taxes seems to reflect such a norm). In the case where government must single out particular individuals by violating their property for public use or public benefit, as long as government is perceived to be keeping up its end of the social contract by acknowledging the norm of reciprocity through the act of compensation, there is less likely to be massive opposition against such government intervention. Having the government compensate owners for the homes it takes is often perceived as treating people fairly by giving them market value for their homes. Failure of government to reimburse people for the homes it seizes is seen as the government not treating people fairly and violating the norms of reciprocity, creating an emotional response of government swindling people and treating them unfairly (Pildes 1996, 2070-2071).

Prosterman and Riedinger (1987) look at different countries to see the various results and reactions that occur when government takes large tracts of land and redistributes them more evenly. What Prosterman and Riedinger show is that the least successful means of taking people's landholdings and giving them to others occurs when government simply redistributes such landholdings without compensating the owners at all. Failure to compensate the landowners creates the most resistance among the legitimate landowners (Prosterman and Riedinger 1987). When compensation is paid, however, even though such compensation fails to reflect the subjective value of land parcels owners, nevertheless, land redistribution policies are more widely accepted and proceed more easily (Pildes 1996, 2071).

The Supreme Court's 5-4 decision in the case of *Kelo vs. City of New London* held that the government could seize private property not just for public use but for any project that could potentially benefit the public. In this specific case, the city government seized a widow's house in order to give the entire area of land to Pfizer to build a new pharmaceutical facility. This decision created more controversy than any other issue decided during the Supreme Court's 2004-2005 term (Lopez and Totah, 2007, 397). Many media outlets criticized the verdict in the *Kelo* case. Numerous media outlets and commentators mentioned how the *Kelo* verdict would lead to a huge increase in rent-seeking and cronyism, essentially putting an end to private property rights in the United States, as Will Collier, writing for *Vodkapundit.com* lamented (Lopez and Totah, 2007, 398). Andrew Sullivan from *Time Magazine* wrote how as a result of the *Kelo* case, government can seize people's homes to give to a Walmart, without giving the land owner fair compensation (Lopez and Totah, 2007, 398). Other media outlets, such as *The Washington Post* echoed similar fears.

The perceived injustice of the *Kelo* decision created a national political backlash in support of greater protections for private property rights (Lopez, Jewell, and Campbell 2008, 1-2). Such a "backlash and spotlight" effect (where public opinion shifted toward more support of private property owners, and therefore states where fear of negative publicity and legal battles) has caused some state legislatures to put greater restrictions on the use of eminent domain in order to assuage such popular disapproval (Lopez and Totah, 2007, 398).

After *Kelo*, several pollsters and newspapers analyzed public sentiment, which was found to be overwhelmingly negative. In many online polls, more than 90% of those polled, as well as 68% of registered voters, disagreed with the *Kelo* ruling (Lopez and Totah, 2007, 405). In order to calm the flames, House majority leader Tom DeLay called *Kelo* a horrible decision, and the House passed a resolution by a vote of 365 to 33 to express grave disapproval of the Supreme Court's ruling (Lopez and Totah, 2007, 405).

Networks that improve the efficiency of society are a part of social capital (Putnam 1993, 167). For Putnam, the two main elements of social capital are networks and trust (Fu, 2004, 9). The *Kelo* ruling has led to an increase in bridging social capital, since the *Kelo* decision is so blatantly a violation of property rights and a form of rent-seeking where politicians can redistribute people's homes to their constituents, there is a broader network supporting private property owners.

Bridging social capital was invested by advocacy groups who took their complaints to the media, who reported the negative feelings the *Kelo* ruling caused. As a response, many states drafted bills limiting the powers of eminent domain. Utah and Nevada's legislatures limited the use of eminent domain in response to the *Kelo* decision and as of June 15th 2006, bills limiting the powers of eminent domain have been considered in forty-three states, passed in twenty-seven of them, and bills have been enacted in eighteen of those states in response to the public outcry

(Lopez and Totah 2007, 406). Also in response to public outcry, in 2004, the Michigan Supreme Court overturned the 1981 *Poletown* decision, which had allowed Detroit to transfer an entire working-class neighborhood to General Motors in order to build a Cadillac plant (Lopez and Totah 2007, 406).

Public outcry against the *Kelo* decision, while not leading to narrowing the powers of eminent domain in all states, has diminished its power in some states. California, for example, didn't update its Takings Clause following the *Kelo* ruling, and Florida ended up taking advantage of the *Kelo* decision to change their laws in order to further broaden the use of eminent domain.

Lopez, Jewell, and Campbell point out that the first states to quickly update their laws after the *Kelo* ruling in order to restrict the use of eminent domain are those states with more economic freedom, greater value of new housing construction, and less racial and income inequality (Lopez, Jewell, and Campbell 2008, 1). Lopez, et al. also point out that in most instances, the changing of takings powers was done more for symbolic purposes, to signal to the citizenry that the state legislatures are responding to the backlash by drafting bills and new legislation, protecting homeowners from having their homes seized by the government. In order to know if the new laws are designed for symbolic purposes or to actually limit the power of the state in the cases of eminent domain, we must analyze the language of the new laws. In general, laws that do little to restrict takings power include vague and encompassing definitions for "blight" and "public use," whereas strong laws that meaningfully restrict takings for private use (and are not merely an empty symbolic gesture) contain some sort of prohibition on land development takings, without much in the law granting exceptions or loopholes (Lopez, Jewell, and Campbell 2008, 9).

Lopez, Jewell, and Campbell point out how beginning in the late 1800's, court cases have incrementally expanded takings powers, and since the 1980's, local governments have taken a gradually increased role in central planning and regional development (Lopez, Jewell, and Campbell 2008, 4). The idea that private land developers have been able to successfully collude with legislative bodies in order to take property from private property owners and have it transferred to them is not a recent discovery. Yet, while legislative bodies have been gradually increasing the power of eminent domain and the takings clause, before Kelo, it had been over 50 years since the last major Supreme Court case involving redistributing the land holdings of large number of property owners for the private gain of developers, instead of for "public use" (Lopez, Jewell, and Campbell 2008, 5). It being so long until such a case was brought to the Supreme Court is what made the *Kelo* ruling come as a shock and may be a causal factor in spurring such controversy and creating such a backlash. Perhaps if the cultural climate was more used to being aware of the rent-seeking activity of land developers, people would be used to it, and less of a backlash would occur.

It is important to point out that status quo politics, more than any actual protection for homeowners, is a common response to the *Kelo* verdict. Since backlash is often short-lived, many legislatures may draft laws in order to appear to calm the tempers without offering any real protection. *"Thus, a new law does not necessarily mean that development takings have been restricted. Legislators may wish to obfuscate the effects of the new laws in order to avoid appearances of corruption"* (Boylan and Long 2003).

Abraham Lincoln supposedly said, *"The best way to get a bad law repealed is to enforce it strictly."* Successful tyrants are able to seize political power and take away people's rights because they do so gradually. Human beings are much like the frogs who jump out of hot water when the flame is turned on high. The best way to cook a frog isn't to immediately put the flame on high, but to put the flame on low and slowly increase the temperature until the frog is unaware he is being cooked. Human beings are much the same way. New pieces of legislation that so blatantly violate the norms of society are likely to create great resistance and be rejected. The way to get a piece of legislation passed in order to violate the norms of society is to do so subtly and gradually, where each piece of individual legislation seems reasonable, or at least not hostile enough to create strong resistance. Legislative laws that immediately try to upend societal expectations where the flame is on high, as shown above, are liable to create more pushback than laws which violate property rights (as all eminent domain laws do) moderately and gradually.

A case could be made to vote for the greater of two evils, or at least the politician who most people interpret to be more obviously evil, because the greater evil is liable to be more resisted than the lesser evil. If public opinion recognizes those with political power as a grave threat to them, they are more likely to resist than if public opinion views those with political power as 'better than the alternative' or 'not so bad'. It is for this reason that there is also a dark side to social capital where greater trust can lead to a reduction in skepticism, causing people to be taken advantage of.

Dan Kahan argues for gentle nudges instead of hard shoves when it comes to creating a law that is not consistent with the norms of the society. Kahan argues that those who enforce the law in a less harsh manner are liable to meet less resistance than if the law was harshly enforced. Likewise, Kahan argues that those who enforce a law that is not consistent with currently existing norms feel more comfortable enforcing the law if they do so in a less harsh manner (Kahan 2000, 625). As Kahan points out, gradually increasing the punishment can signal that such acts are met with moral disapproval, and seeing that people are willing to enforce such soft punishments allows the punishments to gradually grow more severe over time, such as in the case of increasing penalties when it comes to illegal narcotics (which began as criticizing those who used drugs, then turned into fines, and only later led to incarceration). If the drug laws started all at once to be met with a severe penalty when the norm against drug use wasn't so strong, such penalties would have caused advocacy groups to speak out and encourage people to resist the law.

Kahan says, *"Had lawmakers attempted to dictate a regulatory regime of this intensity in one fell swoop thirty or...twenty years ago—when public attitudes towards smoking were at best ambivalent—they most certainly would have provoked a...'hard shove' reaction."* Indeed, this is exactly what has happened when regulators have attempted less incremental regulation of smoking. Thus, in the early part of the century, a significant number of American states enacted tobacco prohibitions, which proved utterly ineffective (Kahan 2000, 626). Kahan's main point is that when laws are created that seem to go against a common norm of society, harsh laws are unlikely to be effective, whereas less severe penalties are likely to be enforced. Once penalties, such as shaming or fines are enforced, this signals to people that such actions are met with disapproval and that it is okay for people to speak out against such behaviors. This changes the norm, as people then feel more comfortable speaking out against certain actions, leading to increasing penalties over time. I share Kahan's sentiment that the best way for government legislation to not meet resistance is to increase the penalty gradually so that people are unlikely to resist, rather than to create a harsh penalty all at once. Such a view seems to explain why *Kelo* met with greater resistance than other eminent domain laws, and that is because the ruling came as a harsh surprise that changed the norm of public use to public benefit in one fell swoop.

5. Conclusion

Much like other forms of capital, social capital is invested by entrepreneurs in order to increase their future income. Social capital includes the norms, networks, and levels of trust and reciprocity within a society. As we have seen, government intervention can destroy or alter such social capital by diminishing the levels of trust within a society, such as in the case of urban development or government welfare programs and mandated insurance. If pushed too hard, government intervention can also lead to greater resistance and greater support of the informal norms over government mandates. Government intervention can lead to a change in ideology where a climate of increasing government intervention causes support for favoring government as a solution to solve programs, and people are more likely to trade their liberty for the illusion of safety. There are also transition economies, where government intervention doesn't lead to increased intervention, but at some point leads to a move towards a more market-oriented society.

As shown above, there are some important implications when it comes to social capital and government intervention. One is that social capital can be created by entrepreneurs who attempt to change the rules of the game and be opinion molders, leading to a change in norms. While Boettke and Coyne (2004) explain how the entrepreneur is the agent of social and cultural change in different settings, such as the market, the society, and in the political arena, Boettke and Coyne (2003) also point out how the entrepreneur is not the cause of economic development since certain institutions must be in place where the entrepreneur is free to be able to invest, create, and be the agent of social and cultural change. In a society with an abundance of capital and natural resources where heavy government intervention prohibits the entrepreneur from exploiting the opportunities that exist, the entrepreneur won't succeed at increasing levels of trust and reputations. One must be able to profit from his investment in social capital to be able to make such investments worthwhile. Another implication is that social capital is not one thing, but involves many layers of heterogeneous goods that can be put to different uses, and therefore perhaps another paper can help clarify what distinguishes social capital from asocial capital, or from capital to consumption. Another purpose of my paper is to try to figure out when government rontervention leads to a cycle of ever-increasing government intervention and when it leads to pushback and a consequent reduction in the amount of government intervention in the economy.

Areas of interest for future research should explore what causes an ideology to develop and the role of the entrepreneur in influencing a change in ideology. Do norms differ from ideology, do institutions influence and lead to a change in ideology, or does ideology determine the institutions that exist? Or is there a tradeoff, where it is not so clear whether ideology determines the institutions and norms that exist, or whether the ideology is determined by the institutional setting of the society?

Another area for future research is to try to determine what leads economies to transition from a more socialist society towards a more market driven society? Do other market societies have an influence on transition economies? What role does social capital play in transition economies, and does the case of government introducing a "hard shove" approach instead of gradualism have an influence on weakening public perception of the state, leading to people resisting the state's influence on their lives, causing a society to transition? All these questions would make a good future essay topic. Trying to answer the question of the role that increasing social capital has on ideology may provide some insights into both the positive and negative consequences that increasing social capital can lead to. For example, do increasing levels of trust in a market setting have a spillover effect where people have greater levels of trust and therefore are less skeptical of government, allowing government to take advantages of people's increasing levels of trust by intervening more and more, and meeting less resistance? Or do increasing levels of trust lead to increasing levels of trust in the market society, where people have more trust in market solutions, but greater distrust of government intervention? All these questions would make for a fascinating possible future paper topic.

References

1) Adler, Paul S., and Seok-Woo Kwon. "Social capital: The good, the bad, and the ugly." (2000): 89-115.
2) Arrow, Kenneth J. "Observations on social capital." *Social capital: A multifaceted perspective* (2000): 3-5.
3) Benson, Bruce L. "The spontaneous evolution of commercial law." *Southern Economic Journal* (1989): 644-661.
4) Benson, Bruce L. "The impetus for recognizing private property and adopting ethical behavior in a market economy: Natural law, government law, or evolving self-interest." *The Review of Austrian Economics* 6.2 (1993): 43-80.
5) Benson, Bruce L. "Knowledge, trust and recourse: imperfect substitutes as sources of assurance in emerging economies." *Economic Affairs* 21.1 (2001): 12-17.
6) Berggren, Niclas, and Henrik Jordahl. "Free to trust: Economic freedom and social capital." *Kyklos* 59.2 (2006): 141-169.
7) Boettke, Peter J., and Virgil Henry Storr. "Post-classical political economy: Polity, society and economy in Weber, Mises and Hayek." *American Journal of Economics and Sociology* (2002): 161-191.
8) Boettke, Peter J., and Christopher J. Coyne. *Entrepreneurship and development: Cause or consequence?*. na, 2003.
9) Boettke, Peter J., Christopher J. Coyne, and Peter T. Leeson. "Institutional stickiness and the new development economics." *American journal of economics and sociology* 67.2 (2008): 331-358.
10) Boettke, Peter J., and Christopher J. Coyne. "An entrepreneurial theory of social and cultural change." *Markets and civil society: The European experience in comparative perspective* (2009): 77-103.
11) Bourdieu, Pierre. "The forms of capital Handbook of theory and research for the sociology of education (pp. 241–258)." (1986).

12) Boylan, Richard T., and Cheryl Long. "A survey of state house reporters' perception of public corruption." *State Politics and Policy Quarterly* 3.4 (2003): 420-438.
13) Burt, Ronald S. *Structural holes: The social structure of competition*. Harvard university press, 2009.
14) Campbell, Noel D., Alex Fayman, and Kirk Heriot. "Growth in the Number of Firms and the Economic Freedom Index in a Dynamic Model of the US States." *Journal of Economics and Economic Education Research* 12.2 (2011): 51.
15) Carilli, Anthony M., Christopher J. Coyne, and Peter T. Leeson. "Government intervention and the structure of social capital." *The Review of Austrian Economics* 21.2-3 (2008): 209-218.
16) Chalupnicek, Pavel. "The CAPITAL in Social Capital: An Austrian Perspective." *American Journal of Economics and Sociology* 69.4 (2010): 1230-1250.
17) Chalupníček, Pavel, and Lukáš Dvořák. "Health insurance before the welfare state: the destruction of self-help by state intervention." *The Independent Review* 13.3 (2009): 367-387.
18) Chamlee-Wright, Emily. "The structure of social capital: An Austrian perspective on its nature and development." *Review of Political Economy* 20.1 (2008): 41-58.
19) Coleman, James S. "Social capital in the creation of human capital." *American journal of sociology* (1988): S95-S120.
20) Coyne, Christopher J. "The institutional prerequisites for post-conflict reconstruction." *The Review of Austrian Economics* 18.3-4 (2005): 325-342.
21) Fine, Ben. "Social capital and capitalist economies." *South-Eastern Europe Journal of Economics* 2.1 (2015).
22) Fu, Qianhong. *Trust, social capital, and organizational effectiveness*. Diss. Virginia Polytechnic Institute and State University, 2004.

23) Fukuyama, Francis. "Social capital, civil society and development." *Third world quarterly* 22.1 (2001): 7-20.

24) Glazer, Nathan. *The limits of social policy.* Harvard University Press, 1988

25) Granovetter, Mark. "Economic action and social structure: The problem of embeddedness." *American journal of sociology* (1985): 481-510.

26) Gruber, Jonathan, and Daniel M. Hungerman. "Faith-based charity and crowd-out during the great depression." *Journal of Public Economics* 91.5 (2007): 1043-1069.

27) Hayek, Friedrich August. "The use of knowledge in society." *The American economic review* 35.4 (1945): 519-530.

28) Hayek, F. A. *Law, legislation and liberty: a new statement of the liberal principles of justice and political economy, v. 1: Rules and order.* London: Routledge, 1973.

29) Higgs, Robert. *Crisis and Leviathan: Critical episodes in the growth of American government.* Oxford University Press, USA, 1989.

30) Ikeda, Sanford. "The Role of" Social Capital" in the Market Process." *Journal des Economistes et des Etudes Humaines* 12.2 (2002).

31) Ikeda, Sanford. *Dynamics of the mixed economy: Toward a theory of interventionism.* Routledge, 2002.

32) Ikeda, Sanford. "Urban interventionism and local knowledge." *The review of Austrian economics* 17.2-3 (2004): 247-264.

33) Ikeda, Sanford. "The meaning of "social capital" as it relates to the market process." *The Review of Austrian Economics* 21.2-3 (2008): 167-182.

34) Jacobs, Jane. *The death and life of great American cities.* Vintage, 1961.

35) Kahan, Dan M. "Gentle nudges vs. hard shoves: Solving the sticky norms problem." *The University of Chicago Law Review* (2000): 607-645.

36) Kaplow, Louis. "An economic analysis of legal transitions." *Harvard Law Review* (1986): 509-617.

37) Klein, Daniel B. "Quality-and-Safety Assurance: How Voluntary Social Processes Remedy Their Own Shortcomings." *The Independent Review* 2.4 (1998): 537-555.
38) Klein, Daniel B., Asymmetric Interpretations. Journal des Economistes et des Etudes Humaines, pp. 23-29, March 2002. Available at SSRN: https://ssrn.com/abstract=465081
39) Klein, Daniel B. *Knowledge and coordination: a liberal interpretation.* Oxford University Press, 2011.
40) Leeson, Peter T. "Endogenizing fractionalization." *Journal of institutional economics* 1.01 (2005): 75-98.
41) Leeson, Peter T. "Balkanization and assimilation: Examining the effects of state-created homogeneity." *Review of Social Economy* 65.2 (2007): 141-164.
42) Leeson, Peter T. "Social distance and self-enforcing exchange." *The Journal of Legal Studies* 37.1 (2008): 161-188.
43) Leeson, Peter T., and Christopher J. Coyne. "Wisdom, alterability, and social rules." *Managerial and Decision Economics* 33.5-6 (2012): 441-451.
44) Lewin, Peter. "Time, change and complexity: Ludwig M. Lachmann's contributions to the theory of capital." *Advances in Austrian Economics.* 1996.
45) Lewis, Paul A. "18 Structure and agency in economic analysis: the case of Austrian economics and the material embeddedness of socio-economic life." *The Elgar Companion to Economics and Philosophy* (2004): 364.
46) Lewis, Paul, and Emily Chamlee-Wright. "Social embeddedness, social capital and the market process: An introduction to the special issue on Austrian economics, economic sociology and social capital." *The Review of Austrian Economics* 21.2 (2008): 107-118.f
47) López, Edward J., and Sasha M. Totah. "Kelo and its discontents: The worst (or best?) thing to happen to property rights." *The Independent Review* 11.3 (2007): 397-416.

48) Lopez, Edward J., R. Todd Jewell, and Noel D. Campbell. "Pass a law, any law, fast! State legislative responses to the Kelo backlash." *Review of Law & Economics* 5.1 (2009): 101-135.

49) Meadowcroft, John, and Mark Pennington. "Bonding and bridging: Social capital and the communitarian critique of liberal markets." *The Review of Austrian Economics* 21.2-3 (2008): 119-133.

50) Mises, Ludwig von. *Human action.* Ludwig von Mises Institute, 1949.

51) Murray, Charles A. *Losing ground: American social policy, 1950-1980.* Basic books, 1984.

52) Pejovich, Svetozar. "The effects of the interaction of formal and informal institutions on social stability and economic development." *Journal of Markets and Morality* 2.2 (1999).

53) Pennington, Mark. "Citizen Participation, the-Knowledge Problem-and Urban Land Use Planning: An Austrian Perspective on Institutional Choice." *The Review of Austrian Economics* 17.2-3 (2004): 213-231.

54) Pildes, Richard H. "The destruction of social capital through law." *University of Pennsylvania Law Review* 144.5 (1996): 2055-2077.

55) Posner, Eric A. "Symbols, signals, and social norms in politics and the law." *The Journal of Legal Studies* 27.S2 (1998): 765-797.

56) Prosterman, Roy L. Riedinger, Jeffrey M. Roy L. Prosterman, and Jeffrey M. Riedinger. *Land reform and democratic development.* No. 333.32 P7. 1987.

57) Putnam, Robert D. "Bowling alone: America's declining social capital." *Journal of democracy* 6.1 (1995): 65-78.

58) Putnam, Robert D. "Bowling alone: America's declining social capital." *Culture and Politics.* Palgrave Macmillan US, 2000. 223-234.

59) Siisiainen, Martti. "Two concepts of social capital: Bourdieu vs. Putnam." *International Journal of Contemporary Sociology* 40.2 (2003): 183-204.

60) Smith, Adam. *An Inquiry Into the Nature and Causes of the Wealth of Nations*, 1976, Oxford University Press.
61) Solow, Robert M. "Notes on social capital and economic performance." *Social capital: A multifaceted perspective* 6.10 (2000).
62) Westlund, Hans. "Implications of social capital for business in the knowledge economy: theoretical considerations." *International Forum on Economic Implication of Social Capital—, held by the Economic and Social Research Institute, Cabinet Office, Japan, in Tokyo on 24th and 25th March*. 2003.
63) Westlund, Hans, and Roger Bolton. "Local social capital and entrepreneurship." *Small business economics* 21.2 (2003): 77–113.
64) Wildavsky, Aaron B. *Searching for safety*. Vol. 10. Transaction publishers, 1988.

Sticky Prices are a Natural Part of the Market

According to Yeager, an excess demand for money is the root cause of a depression. There is no general overproduction of goods and services because goods and services are paid for under a common medium of exchange—money—and there is some price at which demand and supply intersect. However, unlike other goods and services, money has no common medium of exchange of its own, and there is therefore no price at which the demand and supply of money are equal. According to Yeager, since money has no single price at which to clear the market, there can be an excess demand or an excess supply of money. Prices are considered sticky because in cases where people want to increase their money balances and hold more money than is currently in existence, there is a disequilibrium for money. As Yeager states, *"Say's law overlooks monetary disequilibrium. If people on the whole are trying to add more money to their cash balances than is being added to the total money stock (or are trying to maintain their cash balances when the money stock is shrinking), they are trying to sell more goods and labor than are being bought. If people on the whole are unwilling to add as much money to their total cash balances as is being added to the total money stock (or are trying to reduce their cash balances when the money stock is not shrinking), they are trying to buy more goods and labor than are being offered"* (Yeager 1997, 5).

Because it is possible for people taken together to want to increase their cash balances and demand more money than the total money stock, this leads to an excess demand for money. Because prices are measured in terms of money, prices can be sticky because there are cases where the demand to hold money may not instantaneously match the available supply. When there is an excess demand for money, there is an excess supply of goods, so prices are sticky downward where people try to build up their real money balances, but there is too little demand for goods and services to sell them all at the existing prices which leads to unsold inventories and cutbacks in production, along with price cuts.

While Yeager advocated deliberately managing money to keep its supply and demand in equilibrium and to have price level stability, even Yeager admits that getting rid of all price stickiness would not prevent the problems caused by sticky prices: *"An economy beset by monetary disturbances faces a catch 22: It is damned whether or not it exhibits great flexibility of wages and prices"* (Greenfield and Yeager 1989, 409-410).

1. Critique: Sticky prices are not a market problem because the supply of money is determined by the average price of money

The problem of there being an excess demand for money where markets can't clear and where there is a general glut of unsold inventories, so long as price cuts haven't occurred is mainly a result of there not being an endogenous supply of money, which is a result of being under a fiat standard due to government monopolizing the supply. Under a fiat system in which the government monopolizes the money supply, the increase in the demand for money is not determined by market forces. It is therefore not a result of market imperfections, but of government intervention. If the government did not prevent competition and allowed the money to be under a commodity standard then the price mechanism would serve as the vehicle determining when there should be an increase in the money supply. Under a commodity money market, an excess demand for money leads to a fall in prices and an increase in the money supply by entrepreneurs who believe it's worth investing in the resources to increase the money supply (such as the resources needed to extract more gold—the probable commodity money).

As Hendrickson (2015, 5) explains, the reduction in trade that occurs as a result of a discrepancy between actual and desired money balances (such as having an excess demand for money) could be eliminated by increasing the supply of money to bring the supply and demand for money back to monetary equilibrium. Hendrickson states that economic agents lack the ability to signal to others that there is a discrepancy between real and desired money balances and in the absence of private note issuance, there is no way to facilitate such trade even if such a mechanism did exist (2015, 5). Hendrickson mentions that free bankers, such as Selgin (1988) advocate a free banking system (i.e. free from government regulation) in which banks could increase the money supply by having the banks increase their bank notes whenever there is monetary disequilibrium and therefore the profit motive of the market would serve as a signaling device to increase the money supply until the supply of money equaled the demand for money. Therefore, in the absence of government monopolization of the money supply, the supply of money would be determined by market demand and not by government policy.

The idea of price stickiness as something that needs correction seems to imply that price stickiness is a type of market failure that ought to be corrected. In the case of free bankers such as Selgin, Yeager, and Larry White, the money supply should equal the demand for money. So, in order to keep spending stable (or steady), banks should engage in fractional reserve banking in order to increase the supply of money to equal the demand. Such free bankers advocate allowing an increase in the monetary base even under a fiat system. In cases of sticky prices where prices fail to instantly adjust to changes to real preference or demand changes, the money supply should increase to correct for such sticky price imperfections. When prices are sticky and aren't able to fall fast enough to equilibrate the real supply of money and the demand for real cash balances, the public is willing to supply loanable funds but the banking system is not producing investment in response; in such a case, an expansion of the money supply is an appropriate policy, independent of any commodity backing the supply of money (Horowitz 2006, 176). As will be explained further below, increasing the supply of money, even when the market rate is above the natural rate, creates distortions and wealth transfers. Advocating increasing the money supply in such a case, under a fiat system where government monopolizes the money supply, is to advocate government policy instead of allowing prices to naturally adjust. While Horowitz may feel that prices aren't adjusting quickly enough, participants in the market may disagree by the simple fact that they choose to not pay the cost that comes with allowing prices to become unstuck.

My claim is that there is nothing wrong with sticky prices and that they are a natural part of the market. To advocate for any monetary policy is to enter the realm of normative policies instead of explaining economic behavior and phenomena. Economics is a positive, value-free science that describes economic behavior, not a normative, prescriptive field in which the economist advocates changes in economic interactions based on what is preferable according to the economist's point of view. Just as economics doesn't advocate wage controls and does not mandate any particular wage, so too does economics (being value-free) doesn't dictate what the price level should be. By advocating for a flexible money supply when prices are sticky, such economists are saying that one price level is preferable to another price level. Since prices can never be perfectly stable and some price stickiness is inevitable, how does the economist determine whether prices are too sticky or too flexible? In other words, what determines whether there is too much price stickiness or not enough? What is the objective optimal level of prices and who decides? Value-free economics wouldn't have an answer to that, because an optimal price level is not determined by the economist's own values but by the voluntary actions of buyers and sellers.

Money is not neutral and an increase in the money supply benefits some people and makes other people worse off. As Bagus and Howden mention, because of Cantillon effects, any change in the money supply aimed at reducing or eliminating monetary disequilibria in certain areas will not be felt equally in all markets. Some prices that did not cause the original disequilibrium may increase; other prices which did cause it may not be affected by an increase in the money supply (Bagus and Howden 2011, 23). As Bagus and Howden explain, let's assume that both prices A and B are sticky downward. Price A needs to fall due to an increase in the demand for money, but Price A is sticky, so a surplus is the result. Price B is sticky, but has no reason to change its price because the relative demand for the good has simultaneously increased with the increased demand for money. When credit is increased and directed toward good B, this causes its price to increase. Good A's price, however, will still need to decrease in order to be sold. *"Disequilibrium will still persist regardless of the use of credit to counter sticky prices"* (Bagus and Howden 2011, 23).

Steve Horwitz says that *"The key is that the supply of money must be 'right' in order for demand to properly reflect production. If money is not right. then gluts and shortages will occur...If money is in short supply, some producers will be unable to demand, as they will be unable to sell their goods for money, given that it is relatively unavailable. The result will be a glut, as goods and labour sit unsold. Conversely, an excess supply of money will, in the short run, heighten overall purchasing power even though there has been no sustainable increase in production...The eventual result of all of this will be shortages, and the rising prices we associate with excess supplies of money"* (Horowitz 2003, 92).

As Horowitz states above, there seems to be something wrong when there is an excess demand for money because some producers will be unable to sell their goods for money because the money is unavailable, and as a result, there will be sticky prices and unsold goods. I fail to see how the supply of money is not right in this case. It seems that Horowitz is simply inferring that people prefer to increase their cash balances and save instead of buying the goods that producers produce. I see no reason why the preferences of people who decide to "hoard" more money should be sacrificed in order to transfer that money to people who prefer to use the money to buy goods instead. Likewise, it may be possible that producers expect the demand for money to increase in the near future and do not want to sell at the current prices (Bagus and Howden 2011, 19). Such preferred idleness, as Hutt refers to it, may result in a glut where output declines, but this simply reflects the preferences of the firms. Preferred idleness also need not be a result of an excess demand for money but for a variety of other reasons. Preferred idleness merely reflects the wishes of the producers and there is no reason why wanting to hold out for possible future higher prices is considered less legitimate than having to sell the goods at the current prices.

According to Rotemberg (1982, 1190), price stickiness is sometimes a result of consumer preferences because consumers prefer firms that have relatively stable prices and tend to avoid firms with large, frequent price changes.

Horowitz (2006, 171) mentions that no firm would wish to be the first to cut output prices without sufficient certainty of a cut in input prices to offset the probable negative impact on profits. Being the first to cut output prices in such a case is a public good problem where the benefits of being the first to cut prices are dispersed but the costs of doing so are concentrated. A reply to this is that this is what entrepreneurs do. Entrepreneurs are in the business of forecasting and taking risks and those that are able to successfully predict what the consumer wants and successfully predict whether input or output prices will rise or fall will make a profit and those that fail to do so will suffer a loss. One can claim that there is also a first-mover problem in investing in R&D since once knowledge is out there, those who don't engage in spending on research can free-ride off of those that do. Yet, the market often rewards successful firms that engage in such valuable research. Why are cutting output prices if some firms believe input prices may also rise a public good problem the market may solve? Knowledge creation also has what many market interventionists consider concentrated costs and dispersed benefits, yet the market often proves otherwise.

2. Conclusion

In conclusion, sticky prices are a natural part of the market that simply reflects the preferences of consumers and producers and is not a result of any type of market imperfection. When there is monetary disequilibrium and the supply and demand of money are not equal, there is no need to increase the supply of money in order to satisfy an increase in the demand for money in order to prevent unsold inventory from both a willing buyer and seller. As Bagus and Howden clearly state, *"In light of a constant money supply, any increase in cash balances will place downward pressure on prices. As individuals are seeking to increase their real cash balances, this involves a relatively and increasing small amount of nominal holdings due to a decline in the general price level...When the demand for money increases, its purchasing power is bid up and real cash balances automatically increase, thereby satisfying the demand for an increase in real cash holdings. It is not necessary to increase the supply of money to satisfy the increase in demand for real cash balances. An elastic supply of fiduciary media frustrates this very process, by placing upward pressure on the price level (in the case of the goods purchased with the increased money supply)"* (Bagus and Howden 2011, 26).

Any increase in the money supply results in a redistribution of wealth, because money is not neutral and the money spent on the present goods will be cheaper than money spent on future goods. An increase in the money supply benefits early consumers at the expense of future consumers (aka savers). The idea that price stickiness, if a result of natural market forces, is something that ought to be counteracted is mistaken because it ignores the preferences of consumers and producers. While some goods may see their prices adjust almost instantly, this need not be the case for all goods and services. If a producer is unwilling to change their prices immediately, this reflects their preference for wanting to take the risk that prices may rise in the future and to invest in his current goods now by saving them in the hopes of possible higher future prices. It may be the case that the consumer prefers to buy a certain good at the current prices, but if prices are sticky, this may mean that producers are unwilling to sell the good at such a price and there is no reason why the consumer's desire to buy at current prices should take precedence over unwilling producers.

References:

1) Bagus, Philipp, and David Howden. "Monetary equilibrium and price stickiness: Causes, consequences and remedies." *The Review of Austrian Economics* 24.4 (2011): 383-402.
2) Hendrickson, Joshua R. "Monetary equilibrium." *The Review of Austrian Economics* 28.1 (2015): 53-73.
3) Horwitz, Steven. "Say's law of markets: An austrian appreciation." *Two Hundred Years of Say's Law: Essays on Economic Theory's Most Controversial Principle* (2003): 82-98.
4) Horwitz, Steven. "12 Monetary disequilibrium theory and Austrian macroeconomics." *Money and Markets* (2006): 166.
5) Rotemberg, Julio J. "Sticky prices in the United States." *Journal of Political Economy* 90.6 (1982): 1187-1211.
6) Yeager, L. B. "The fluttering veil." *Essays on Monetary Disequilibrium* (1997).
7) Yeager, Leland B., and Robert L. Greenfield. "Can Monetary Disequilibrium Be Eliminate." *Cato J.* 9 (1989): 405.

9 798360 000921